The Insider's Guide to San Diego

The Insider's Guides

The Insider's Guide to New Orleans
Honey Naylor

The Insider's Guide to San Diego
James B. Kelleher

The Insider's Guide to Santa Fe, Third Edition
Bill Jamison and Cheryl Alters Jamison

The Insider's Guide
to
SAN DIEGO

James B. Kelleher

THE HARVARD COMMON PRESS
Boston, Massachusetts

The Harvard Common Press
535 Albany Street
Boston, Massachusetts 02118

Printed in the United States of America

LIBRARY OF CONGRESS CATALOGING-IN-PUBLICATION DATA

Kelleher, James B., 1963-
    The insider's guide to San Diego   /   James B. Kelleher.
       p.   cm.
    Includes index.
    ISBN 1-55832-048-2 : $9.95
    1. San Diego (Calif.)—Guidebooks. I. Title.
  F869.S22K44   1993
  917.94'9850453—dc20   92-38677
                                      CIP

Maps by Jacques Chazaud
Cover design by Jackie Schuman

10 9 8 7 6 5 4 3 2 1

Contents

Maps

San Diego and Vicinity

Acknowledgments
◆◆◆◆◆◆◆◆◆◆◆◆◆◆◆

*T*he *Insider's Guide to San Diego* could not have been written without the help of many people. Friends, family, and colleagues played a crucial role in the project, checking facts, suggesting topics, and grounding my often over-rosy sentiments in reality. I want to express my thanks to them all for the aid, criticism, input, and moral support they provided to me and for which I will never be able to adequately compensate them.

First, a very warm thank you to Julie Castiglia of Waterside Productions for introducing me to the good people at the Harvard Common Press and counseling me throughout this undertaking.

Jackie Shannon, Sam Chammas, and Rosy Vasquez provided assistance of a different sort, contributing crucial tips on San Diego—area attractions for various sections of this book. Special thanks, too, to Ron Quinn, a historian at Old Town San Diego State Historic Park, for the essential information he provided on early California's fascinating history. Jay Smith and Brian Martinet, two good friends, deserve thanks for their input on beaches and hotels respectively. JoAnn Whitney, my dear sister, deserves gratitude for her efforts in the fact-checking and moral-support departments. David and Mary Quimby warrant thanks for the help they provided on the sections of this book that describe San Diego's back country.

Many thanks also to my friend Sharon Whitley. Sharon,

a lifelong San Diegan and *bona fide* Insider, provided invaluable assistance throughout every phase of this project, cheerfully shelving her own writing to check facts and run down essential information for this guide.

I'm also indebted to Dan Rosenberg, my editor at the Harvard Common Press. Few sections of this book did not benefit from Dan's first-rate judgment, eagle-eyed editing, and sensitive but critical reading.

Most of all, I'd like to express my deepest thanks to my wife, Denise, for the enormous patience, devotion, and understanding she displayed as I wrestled with this project. She deserves better.

I dedicate this book to the memory of my parents, William and Helen Kelleher, whom I miss very much.

Where California Begins

F ATHER Junípero Serra was not the first European
to set eyes on San Diego, but his description of the
area, made at the end of a long, hard trek north from
Mexico, is still the best.

After celebrating an inaugural mass on a hilltop overlooking the head of the sparkling bay, the Franciscan
missionary turned to his journal, setting down his
thoughts on the new land stretched out before him. "It is
beautiful to behold," he wrote, looking eastward up the
valley, toward the gently rising mesas and the towering
mountains beyond. "It is a good country, distinctly better
than the old."

Though San Diego has undergone dramatic changes in
the two centuries since Serra penned those words, his
simple portrait continues to capture the city's essence and
allure. Years of development and growth have transformed San Diego into an palm-studded playground for
millions, but the city's natural beauty remains impressive
and largely unchanged. With its stunning coast, small

inland canyons, rolling foothills, wooded mountains and mysterious desert, San Diego continues to be a place of bewitching beauty and heady promise.

The first European to catch a glimpse of this land was Juan Rodríguez Cabrillo, a Portuguese navigator who explored the west coast of North America during the sixteenth century. Like Ponce de León and Giovanni Verrazano before him, Cabrillo plowed the sea, hoping to turn up gold, glory, and a direct route to the Indies. What he found instead was something much more glorious, something infinitely more valuable.

On September 28, 1542, Cabrillo's ships, the *San Salvador* and the *Victoria*, sighted and entered San Diego Bay. Landing at the tip of Point Loma, Cabrillo claimed the area for His Most Catholic Majesty, the King of Spain, naming it *San Miguel* in honor of the saint whose feast day coincided with his arrival. Sixty years later, Sebastián Vizcaíno, yet another Spanish explorer, led an expedition up the California coast. Arriving in Cabrillo's San Miguel on the feast day of St. Didacus (*Diego* in Spanish) of Alcalá, Spain, Vizcaíno wasted no time renaming the port *San Diego de Alcalá.*

The new name stuck. So did the example. Since Vizcaíno rechristened the city and then sailed off into history, San Diego has redefined, rebuilt, and retooled itself time and time again. It has experienced the impositions of three foreign powers, half a dozen Mexican governors, and legions of real-estate speculators, cultists, and fast-food franchisees. Yet throughout it all, the city's inhabitants have held up wonderfully, finding stability and continuity amid confusing, maddening change.

Standing on the steep hill where Serra celebrated his first Mass in California, you discover the secret: the land. Even in turbulent times, the dry, sun-drenched countryside offers promise. Modest hillsides in the city command breathtaking views of the surrounding landscape, filling the heart with a sense of renewal and a sense of possibility. The promise of the land has been felt—and fueled—by travelers and adventurers of all stripes, who have happened upon San Diego, discovered its charms, and stayed. They've unpacked their bags and out have popped the dreams and the quiet strength to try again. For them, San Diego is a good country. It's better than the old. It's a chance to start over. Above all, it's a beautiful thing to behold.

The mild climate conspires with the inviting landscape to ensure that newcomers pursue the land's promise at a cool, relaxed pace. With the average mean temperature hovering in the high 60s all year long, San Diego encourages a leisurely approach to things, and white-hot zeal simply fell out of fashion when the Franciscans left in the 1830s. The only days when the clouds stubbornly hang in the sky come, conveniently enough, during the early summer, when a foggy marine layer moves inland, protecting the city from the ravages of the sun. The delightful weather has provided successive generations of San Diegans with an excuse to relax and enjoy. During the Spanish and Mexican periods, practitioners of this easy-going philosophy were accused of having a *"mañana,"* or "tomorrow" attitude. Today, its devotees are labeled "laid back."

In recent years, San Diego has not escaped the problems challenging other American cities. The ocean to the west, the mountains to the east, and the international border to the south have proved ineffective barriers to the insults of modernity. Still, there's something unconventional and spirited about the city as it confronts the new challenges. The landscape tempts the imagination, forming, you suspect, more than just a backdrop for the future. This is, after all, California. The place where the warm dry air is clarified by soft ocean breezes and those with the desire to look, and the eyes to see, behold dreams and solutions poised on the edge of razor-sharp horizons. California continues to be a good country, distinctly better than the old. And San Diego is where California begins.

PART ONE
••••••••••
UNDERSTANDING
SAN DIEGO

Chapter One
♦♦♦♦♦♦♦♦♦♦♦

The San Diego Heritage

THE FIRST people to feel San Diego's strange pull were the Kumeyaay, members of the Hokan-Siouan family of Indians, who drifted into the region perhaps one thousand years before the first Europeans arrived.

Of course, the Kumeyaay weren't the *first* people to populate the area. That honor belongs to the San Dieguito and La Jolla Indians, who moved into the northern coastal region of San Diego between 10,000 B.C. and 5000 B.C. Yet the Kumeyaay were special nonetheless. For centuries, these nomads had roamed the desert Southwest, moving on whenever their numbers outran the limited resources of wherever they happened to be. The Kumeyaay were, in a word, drifters, and setting down roots was not a pattern of behavior that came easily to them. But when these itchy travelers wandered into San Diego, they were suddenly transformed. The wind whispered it was time to adopt a new lifestyle and that this was the place to do it. So the Kumeyaay people stopped wandering and settled down in the region. They were not the last people to hear

San Diego's captivating whisper. By 1769, there were perhaps four thousand Kumeyaay in the area, living in small groups scattered throughout the county to increase their chances of surviving in the sparse countryside. Unlike their Yuman cousins, who began cultivating crops, the Kumeyaay remained fully dedicated hunters and gatherers, roaming and foraging on the coastal plain and in the rolling back country. Traveling barefoot most of the time, they gathered lambs' celery, sage, currants, and yucca and hunted quail, rabbits and rats. They supplemented this meager diet with regular trips to the bay and tidal pools, where they cast nets to catch small fish, mollusks, and sea birds.

At the center of the Kumeyaay diet was the acorn, which was easily stored and prepared many different ways. Often, the acorns were crushed, creating a flour that was washed and sun-dried repeatedly to remove tannins, then cooked like a pancake. Acorns were also an important part of Kumeyaay people's commerce with neighboring tribes, traded for salt and other items in short supply.

Like its diet, the tribe's clothing and lodging situation was somewhat rudimentary. During most of the year, the men went about naked, adorned only with body paint and perhaps a headdress made of feathers. The women wore little more than skirts, fashioned from willow bark. Because of the area's mild climate and the tribe's on-the-go lifestyle, Kumeyaay huts were simple affairs, erected with poles and covered with dirt and woven grass. On cool evenings, the Kumeyaay donned small furs made from rabbit or deerskin to ward off the chill.

The leisurely pace of Kumeyaay life, coupled with the tribe's reverence for its surroundings, has caused some observers to suggest that San Diego's present-day preference for easygoing pleasures has ancient roots. But life for the Kumeyaay was not always easy and carefree. They fought deadly battles among themselves, often to determine who controlled a particularly bountiful acorn grove. They had violent encounters with outside foes, too; when they prevailed on the battlefield, the Kumeyaay would scalp their conquered foes—ears and all—and then celebrate their good fortune by drinking huge amounts of fermented jimsonweed and dancing around a campfire, taking turns wearing the bloody trophy. They also ate grasshoppers—lots of them. Clearly, any missionary who found himself among the Kumeyaay had his work cut out for him.

The Franciscan padres who arrived in San Diego with Father Junípero Serra in July of 1769 suspected as much. While Serra penned passages extolling San Diego's breathtaking scenery and dizzying potential, his colleagues groused bitterly about the Kumeyaay, whom they called "*Diegueños*" after *La Mision de San Diego de Alcalá*. One Franciscan described the Diegueños as "vile, ugly, dirty, careless, smutty and flat-faced." Some of his colleagues were even less flattering. The natives resisted the missionaries' every attempt to incorporate them into the mission. Unlike the Indians around *La Mision de San Luis Rey de Francia* (dubbed the "*Luiseños*" by the Spaniards), the Diegueños frustrated all early efforts to get them to accept the faith.

During Serra's first year in San Diego, the mission recorded no baptisms. Though the conversion business picked up later on, the Diegueños could, on occasion, still put up a fight. In 1775, they staged a violent uprising against the Spanish, putting the mission to flames, killing Father Luis Jayme (the only Franciscan to die in the effort to Christianize California's Indians), and running off with two religious paintings. Things actually got worse for the missionaries before they got better, as the tiny Spanish mission and garrison experienced one setback after another.

Fortunately for Spain, adversity did little to diminish the zeal of Junípero Serra, the rugged leader of the Spanish missionaries in California. Sent north by Spain's inspector general in Mexico to establish settlements in Upper California that would check growing Russian influence in the area, Serra made the long and arduous journey on foot. After trudging through the desolate frontier of Lower California for weeks, he finally met up with fellow members of the expedition at the Kumeyaay village of Kosi, near present-day San Diego. While other missionaries headed north to set up missions and blaze *El Camino Real* (Span., the royal road), Serra remained in San Diego. After raising a cross on a hill overlooking Kosi, he marched down to the village and challenged the Diegueños' graven images to a fist fight.

In the end, Serra won. Before La Mision de San Diego de Alcalá was closed in the early 1830s, the Franciscans had baptized over six thousand Indians and were obliged to open an *asistencia*, or chapel, in the Santa Ysabel Valley. Serra's secret was his simple piety. As he worked to implant a Christian civilization in Upper California, the gray-robed padre never forgot that his task was an opportunity, not to be carried out with force. Serra's concern for the Diegueños was shown in many ways, not the least of which was his willingness, in 1774, to move the mission from Presidio Hill to *La Cañada de San Diego* (today's Mission Valley) to insert a little distance between the impressionable Indians and the rough, spiritually suspect Spanish soldiers who manned the fort.

Although the Diegueños were not easily harnessed to the wagon of Christianity, Serra coaxed them into the faith by making it intelligible and intriguing. Using bullfights in the presidio square and edifying plays in the mission chapel (featuring plenty of swordplay and corpses), Serra gave Christianity a bloody veneer the Indians found appealing. During his years in California, Serra established nine thriving missions. Using techniques Serra pioneered, his successors were able to establish 13 more.

During its early years, San Diego was a neglected garrison town on the edge of the Spanish empire and the soldiers and padres who found themselves here were compelled to become largely self-sufficient. They planted olives, pears, and pomegranates to subsist on when the provisioning ships from Mexico didn't arrive—which was most of the time—and they began raising cattle for their hides and tallow. They encouraged the Diegueños to use their hunting skills to trap sea otters and other fur-bearing animals. As a result, the Spaniards were always in a strong trading position when passing merchant ships sailed into San Diego Bay. In between such visits, life was dull and hard—a routine circumscribed by the cross and the sword. Although domestic morality and family rituals made a welcome appearance in the outpost after Serra convinced the authorities to permit wives and children to accompany soldiers to the area, most Spaniards in San Diego looked forward to the day when they could return home.

Gradually however, the rugged, promising beauty of San Diego began to claim Spanish hearts. By the early nineteenth century, soldiers posted to the town started retiring in the area, building small adobe houses down the hill from the presidio in what today is called Old Town. In time, the collection of simple homes became a *pueblo*, or village. As in all Spanish pueblos, life was sleepy and relaxed, enlivened by the occasional *fiesta*, wedding, feast day, or holiday.

The most important festival in San Diego during both the Spanish and Mexican periods was the Feast of the Immaculate Conception, or *La Fiesta de la Patrona*, held on December 8 each year to honor the town's patroness, the Virgin Mary. How a settlement named for St. Didacus of Alcalá, Spain, came to view the Holy Mother as its civic benefactress remains something of a mystery. After all, the other California mission towns considered their namesakes their patrons and reserved the biggest fiestas for them. At least one researcher has suggested that the answer lies in the art spirited away by the Diegueños when they sacked the mission in 1775. According to this theory, the original mission chapel prominently displayed an altar-sized statue of the Immaculate Conception, which simply overshadowed a smaller portrait of San Diego de Alcalá hanging on an adjacent wall. The statue, so the theory goes, quickly became the central symbol of the mission in the eyes of the Diegueños and Spaniards who worshiped there, and it remained the dominating icon in worshipers' minds long after the Diegueños ran off with it. Not wanting to extinguish this flicker of religious enthusiasm—be it ever so flawed—the Franciscans went along with it.

As San Diego grew, it continued to celebrate La Fiesta de la Patrona. One American who found himself here during the 1830s outlined the festival's events:

> Wednesday next the 8th . . . is the feast of the Conception of the Virgin Mary. This day will be set apart by the Native Californians as one of general rejoicing and merry making. The whole of the Plaza has been fenced in for the purpose of having a Bull Fight in the afternoon as soon as the church ceremonies are completed; the whole will conclude with a social Ball, to be given at the house of Don Juan Bandini.

Though Don Juan Bandini was an Italian by birth, his name is inseparable from San Diego's turbulent history under Mexican rule. The isolated tranquility of the Spanish period gave way to the delightful madness of Juan Bandini and the Mexican period in 1821, when Lower California won its independence from Spain and declared sovereignty over Upper California. In the far-flung missions, presidios, and pueblos between San Diego and San Francisco, where isolation, poor communications, and official neglect had fostered a sense of independence, settlers greeted the news that they were now citizens of Mexico with an appropriate amount of leeriness. In San Diego, the padres and soldiers raised the new flag, swore allegiance to the new government and settled back into their old routine, hoping they'd enjoy the same benign neglect under Mexican rule that they'd enjoyed under Spanish rule.

First appearances suggested that would indeed be the case. A new Mexican administrative order grafted itself onto the existing political structures and a few minor innovations were introduced. San Diego got its first *alcalde* (mayor) during the period. But locals weren't crazy to have thought that things would generally remain the way they'd been under the Spaniards.

They were just mistaken. What San Diegans in fact got were front-row seats to the 25 years of low comedy and high melodrama that was Mexican rule, but precious little in the way of competent government. Anyone seriously interested in knowing why San Diegans are so conservative today should pay careful attention to this period.

The first thing the Mexicans did was to cheat the Indians out of their birthright. They accomplished this by "secularizing" the mission system. As Serra envisioned it, the missions held California in trust: the Indians would get it back once they were up to scratch, religiously speaking. While paying Serra's policy plenty of lip service, the steady stream of shady types who moved into the governor's house in Monterey ignored it in practice, appropriating any land they could get their hands on and parceling it out to cousins, allies, and political cronies. Because the mission lands were the most prosperous and well-developed in Southern California, the move to secularize them, as Carey McWilliams pointed out, "degenerated into a mad scramble to loot" and the rights of the Indians "went completely by the board." Those Indians who didn't retreat into the back country were quickly rounded up and used by the Mexicans as peon laborers.

The second thing the Mexicans did was to transform easygoing Spanish California into a political soap opera. Hotheaded factions in the south, known as *abajeños* or *sureños* (Span., lower or southern people), were forever feuding with hotheaded factions in the north, known as the *arribeños* or *norteños* (upper or northern people), hatching plots and counterplots at the drop of a *sombrero*. San Diegans were especially well placed to view all the bickering, intrigue, and treachery, since a good deal of the shenanigans were dreamed up in the San Diego home of Señor Bandini.

The theatrics got off to a fine start in 1825, when José Mariá Echeandía, California's second Mexican governor, moved the provincial capital from Monterey to San Diego because, he said, southern women were more attractive. This naturally offended the women of Northern California, who wasted no time bullying their husbands into open rebellion. Echeandía ruthlessly put down the revolt in Monterey and then returned to San Diego, where he settled into his office routine by giving land to his friends, jailing his enemies, and mistreating any gringos unlucky enough to land in San Diego.

Thus began the succession of uprisings and flip-flops that were the hallmark of Mexican rule. Echeandía's successor, Manuel Victoria, removed the capital to Monterey, much to the delight of Northerners, and then returned to the business of rewarding his friends and exiling his enemies. If you measure a Mexican governor's success in California by the number of conspiracies and plots his rule fostered, then the highhanded Victoria was an enormous success.

In 1831, Juan Bandini cooked up a plot to oust Victoria. The scheme managed to fail and succeed at the same time. With two hundred men, Bandini marched from San Diego to Los Angeles, where Victoria rushed to meet him with an anemic platoon of twenty exhausted irregulars. After Victoria and Bandini exchanged verbal taunts, their "armies" clashed. Within minutes, Victoria's vastly outnumbered contingent drove the rebel force from the field. Victoria celebrated his victory by retreating to a nearby mission; then, in perfect keeping with the topsy-turvy logic of the province, he handed the reins of power to Pio Pico, Bandini's neighbor in San Diego and a co-conspirator in the plot. Pico's sudden promotion sparked an entirely new revolt—this time in Los Angeles—and within twenty days he was out of office. When he finally returned to power in early 1846, Pico kept up the traditions established by his predecessors, deeding thousands of square miles of California to relatives and political cronies. In his last act as governor, Pico granted himself over 130,000 acres of prime land northeast of San Diego.

The curtain didn't come down on this confusing comic-opera until well after the United States invaded California during the Mexican-American War. When General Stephen Kearny and his troops beat a hasty retreat to San Diego after a disastrous skirmish with Pico's army near San Pasqual in 1846, they were welcomed and comforted by a number of the city's leading citizens, including Juan Bandini, Pico's erstwhile ally. It's easy to ridicule the chaos of the Mexican period, but San Diego's history would be flat and colorless without it.

The town's Mexican years came to an abrupt end on July 26, 1846, when the U.S. warship *Cyane* sailed into San Diego Bay bristling with troops looking for a fight. They didn't get one. After an advance party marched to the town square and raised an American flag—provided by Juan Bandini himself and reportedly sewn from old muslins by his daughters—San Diegans celebrated their conquerors' arrival with a grand fiesta.

There was plenty of reason to celebrate. While the Mexicans devoted much time and energy to conspiracies and rebellions to seize the levers of power in California, they did little to maintain, let alone improve, the province. This was especially true in San Diego, where just about everything was in a shambles. The once-proud presidio stood abandoned and decayed. Those bits of the old fort that were salvageable had been removed long ago by various Mexican officials, sold to pay their salaries. There wasn't even a proper *asistencia* for miles around, and San Diegans were forced to celebrate Mass in the large adobe home of Don Jose Antonio Estudillo.

By shutting down the mission system and deeding much of the land to unscrupulous *rancheros*, the Mexicans also created huge problems for the local Indians. Under Spanish tutelage, Diegueño culture and society dissolved, leaving large numbers of Indians under the care and control of the Franciscans. Yet for all their weaknesses, the Franciscans were saints compared to the Mexicans who followed, introducing the Diegueños to a form of communal agriculture that was comprehensible and productive. True, the missions may not have been havens of happiness and contentment, but once they were secularized the Diegueños were left naked and vulnerable to criminal mistreatment by the Mexicans. Some Indians fled to the back country of San Diego County, where they gleaned a poor existence from the terrain and grew increasingly bitter and restive. Many more gravitated toward the town, where they fell victim to swindlers, thugs, and alcohol. The Indians' frustration with their increasing marginalization led, in 1851, to an uprising near Warner Springs. The rebellion failed miserably and all the ringleaders were subsequently caught and executed.

Fortunately, this was not the only legacy of Mexican rule. During the 1830s and '40s, the trade in cow hides boomed in San Diego, thanks largely to Mexican customs officials who had little interest in enforcing the province's strict import-export laws. The La Playa area on the western side of Point Loma was dotted with slaughterhouses and hide huts, where the skins, or "California banknotes" as they were called, were dried and cured before being loaded onto Yankee ships and transported to shoe factories in New England. Suddenly the center of the hide trade in the Western Hemisphere, San Diego lost some of its gentleness, but the city prospered and grew in the bargain.

The surrounding canyons and mesas lost little of their charm as a result of the new business. Captain John C. Fremont, who helped secure California during the Mexican-American War and established friendships with Bandini and Estudillo in the process, spent some time in San Diego after the conflict. Looking over the small farms beneath present-day Mission Hills, Fremont wrote:

> Among the arid, brush-covered hills south of San Diego, we found a little valley converted by a single spring into crowded gardens, where pears, peaches, quinces, pomegranates, grapes, olives and other fruits grew luxuriantly together. This southern frontier of Upper California seems eminently adapted to the cultivation of the vine and the olive.

Although the vine has taken root in the minds of farmers in the northeastern section of the county only quite recently, other forms of truck produce, like avocados, lemons, strawberries, and cut flowers, remained mainstays in the region. Today, the agricultural industry continues to be an important part of San Diego's economic base, ranking fourth behind the military, manufacturing, and tourism.

During the first few decades of the American period,

San Diego grew slowly if it grew at all. The real action during the 1850s and '60s was in the rough boom towns of the California gold rush and the battlegrounds of the American Civil War. Like the rest of Southern California, San Diego remained a largely isolated, Spanish-speaking place, largely unchanged by the annexation.

In the meantime, Old Town faced its own challenges. Located four miles from the harbor, where the hide trade and, for a short time, a robust whale-oil industry were centered, Old Town was isolated from the city's growing connection to the ocean. During the 1850s, a mild speculative frenzy gripped the city, as first La Playa and then William Heath Davis's "New Town" were touted as the new centers of San Diego. Enough San Diegans remained attached to Old Town, however, to forestall any mass exodus for the time being. Throughout the 1850s and '60s, San Diego continued to be a very clannish town, where newcomers were typically absorbed into the community through marriage before they could do too much damage.

In the end, the urge to abandon Old Town came from an outsider who had no interest in assimilating into old San Diego. He was Alonzo Erastus Horton, a shrewd Yankee businessman with a keen eye for business. Arriving in Old Town in 1867, Horton could barely contain his scorn. He took one look around the crude mud huts and decided they simply wouldn't do. "I would not give you five dollars for a deed to the whole of it," Horton wrote. "I would not take it as a gift. It doesn't lie right. Never in the world can you have a city here."

Horton guessed—quite rightly as it turned out—that the harbor would be San Diego's economic strength and that any railroad coming into the city would pass by Old Town and make a beeline for the water. The city fathers didn't know what to make of this excitable Yankee, who prattled on about The Future, Progress, and whatnot. He seemed, quite frankly, a little *loco*.

So when Horton offered them $265 for some apparently worthless scrub, miles south of Old Town, the city fathers jumped at the deal, thinking this at least would get the annoying man out of their hair. Within weeks, Horton had the land, located just southeast of present-day downtown, platted into 226 blocks and up for sale. Sensational advertisements, touting the development as the next New York, were placed in newspapers up and down the West Coast. Thousands of newcomers came to "Horton's Addition," igniting a building boom that resulted in the construction of hundreds of New England–style bungalows in the area and dramatically shifted attention away from sleepy Old Town. As the locus of commerce shifted to Horton's development, Old Town languished. In 1872, a fire raced through one of Old Town's few remaining flourishing blocks. Although only three buildings were destroyed, the blaze gutted the area's hopes, forcing even the stubbornest advocates of Old Town to call it quits.

The success of Horton's New Town aroused a huge amount of speculative interest in San Diego, setting off a series of frenzied real-estate booms and busts during the next two decades. Between 1880 and 1887, the city's population soared from 2,500 to more than 40,000. Tens of thousands of newcomers converged on the city via the new railroad connections. Doubtless, some of them were drawn by San Diego's beauty and promise, but many more were lured by the prospect of easy money. The speculation became so feverish at times that buyers frequently bought land—and sold it—without ever inspecting it. Impressive office buildings and neo-Gothic residences were hastily built in downtown and the surrounding hills to accommodate the people who flocked

into the city from the East, but the explosive growth soon
fizzled out. When the overheated market finally cooled in
1888, and land prices tumbled, thousands fled the city.
By 1890, San Diego's population had shrunk to a mere
16,000 souls.

Since then, the city has enjoyed stable growth and development. The 1915 Panama-California Exposition in Balboa Park introduced hundreds of thousands of visitors to
the city. Many later returned to live out their retirement
years. These retirees were a stable, affluent, and conservative group, with plenty of time on their hands and a feisty
willingness to battle developers, speculators, and flimflam
artists for control of the city's future. Like so many long-
time residents, these gray-clipped newcomers were reluctant to see San Diego grow too wildly and they resisted
"improvements" and policies that seemed likely to
threaten the city's quality of life.

Some boosters complained that this desire to preserve
San Diego's easygoing charm thwarted positive growth
and change. But progress and change came anyway. During the 1880s, fishermen from the Azores and Madeira
Islands had moved to San Diego, quickly establishing a
tight-knit Portuguese community on Point Loma and a
reputation for skill on the high seas. By the 1950s, these
fiercely independent men were operating a huge fleet of
tuna boats, or seiners, from San Diego Harbor, providing
eighty percent of the world's catch and over fifteen thousand local jobs.

In 1907, the U.S. Navy opened a small coaling station
on Point Loma, establishing a presence in the city that has
grown steadily ever since. In the early days, the Navy's
economic impact seemed to be confined to the "Stingaree," San Diego's notorious red-light district (near the
present-day site of the Convention Center), which lured
sailors with its bars, brothels, and opium dens. In later

years, the U.S. military's contributions to the city were more widespread and wholesome, as the Balboa Naval Hospital, the Marine Corps Recruit Depot, and North Island Naval Air Station were set up here.

During the 1920s and '30s, Hollywood discovered San Diego. Although a galaxy's worth of stars and starlets passed through the city on their way down to the casinos and resorts of Tijuana, Rosarito, and Ensenada, a few celebrities took a shine to the city. Some, like Charlie Chaplin, Greta Garbo, and Mae West, began spending their weekends away from the film colony at local hideaways like La Jolla's La Valencia and Coronado's Hotel del Coronado. Others, like Bing Crosby and Anita Page, spent part or all the year here, building second homes, adding to the local color, and contributing much to the local lore.

In 1934, the Consolidated Aircraft Corporation of Buffalo, New York, moved its factory to San Diego, sealing the city's reputation as the "Air Capital of the United States," a reputation that began with the many pioneering flights made from North Island during the 1910s and '20s. In the preparations for World War II, dozens of other war plants followed Consolidated's lead, swelling the population and rocketing the defense industry into great importance locally. Passing through San Diego in 1940 on his way to the Sea of Cortez, author John Steinbeck beheld a naval city girding itself for war:

All about us war bustled, although we had no war; steel and thunder, powder and men—the men preparing thoughtlessly, like dead men to destroy things. The planes roared over in formation and the submarines were quiet and ominous. The Port of San Diego in that year was loaded with explosives and the means of transporting and depositing them on an enemy as yet undetermined. They knew an enemy would emerge, and when one did, they had explosives to deposit on him.

During the subsequent Cold War years, defense contractors like General Dynamics and Convair pumped out high-tech weaponry, including the Atlas and Tomahawk missiles, from plants in and around the city.

More recently, San Diego has become something of a hothouse for biotechnology research and development. The life sciences first entered San Diego's culture in the 1910s, when Helen Browning Scripps, the newspaper heiress, built and endowed the Scripps Institution of Oceanography in La Jolla. With the opening, in the early 1960s, of the University of California, San Diego, the city's research-friendly reputation was enormously enhanced. From humble beginnings, UCSD has come to assume an important role in the scientific world, and has added stars to the city's biomedical cosmos by attracting Nobel Prize–winning research giants like Harold Urey, Linus Pauling, Francis Crick, and Maria Mayer to the campus.

San Diego first became a world-class research-and-development mecca in 1962, when Jonas Salk, the pioneering virologist who discovered the polio vaccine, founded the Salk Institute for Biological Studies in La Jolla. Since Salk's arrival, the area around UCSD and the Salk Institute has become a Silicon Valley for biomedicine, as researchers and entrepreneurs have rushed into the exclusive neighborhood to work in the supercharged scientific atmosphere. Today, San Diego boasts the fourth-largest concentration of biomedical companies in the country.

San Diego's other important industry continues to be tourism. The city's legendary climate and striking beauty lure over thirty million visitors to the area every year and captivate a good percentage of them once they arrive. They look around at the chaparral-covered hills, the miles of sandy beaches, and the remote back country, and, like the Kumeyaay before them, they're hooked.

As a result, San Diego has grown enormously over the years. It has shed its sleepy image and transformed itself into a bustling, sprawling city with a population as diverse as its landscape. Once confined to the "streetcar suburbs" south of Mission Valley, the city has spread out in every possible direction as newcomers have arrived in ever greater numbers. Many of the new arrivals in recent decades have come from the Midwest, following in the footsteps of their grandparents. Many more have come from Vietnam, China, Mexico, and the Philippines. Their discovery of San Diego has sparked a sometimes acrimonious debate among locals, who ponder the city's future and wonder aloud if the quality of the city's physical environment can be maintained. But while these self-styled "natives" fret about growth and lament the disappearance of some of the city's quiet charm, newcomers, unburdened by the memory of What San Diego Was, discover San Diego As It Is. They fall in love and they never leave.

Chapter Two

•••••••••••

The Desert, the Mountains, the Ocean, and the Freeways

S AN DIEGO'S attractions are numerous. Unfortunately, they're rarely near each other. The first thing anyone should know about San Diego is that it is very, very big.

The loosely knit neighborhoods, communities, and towns that make up San Diego County sprawl out over 4,250 square miles, an area larger than both Delaware and Rhode Island and almost the size of Connecticut.

It begins in San Diego, a city located alongside the largest natural harbor in California. From there, it radiates out in every direction down alleys, surface streets, superhighways and back country roads; up the coast, over the mountains, and down into a haunting desert. If you want to catch more than a glimpse of the vast, varied, and eye-filling Big Picture, you're going to need a car. For better or for worse, San Diego experienced its greatest spurts of growth *after* the automobile was invented. As a result, the city has that decentralized feel characteristic of cities in car-dependent Southern California. Destinations and points of interest tend to be far-flung and quite beyond the limited capacity of San Diego's mass-transit facilities. While the city's Metropolitan Transit Service (MTS) has played an admirable game of catch up in recent years, building the trolley system and establishing limited service to the far reaches of East County—what locals call the eastern part of San Diego County—many spots still wait to be integrated into the public-transportation system. You're going to need a car.

The geographic center of this vast county is Ramona, a modest town in the Santa Maria Valley named for the heroine of Helen Hunt Jackson's novel. But the one hundred square miles that make up the city of San Diego are the center of just about everything else. Position yourself here—physically or mentally—to get a feel for the lay of the land.

San Diego's downtown starts at the edge of the harbor, just east of palm-lined Harbor Drive and south of Lindbergh Field, the airport that serves as entry point for most visitors these days. The city's modest skyline rises as it moves away from the water, until Sixth Avenue, when the high-rises end abruptly. The major road bisecting downtown is Broadway, which runs from the shimmering harborside up into Golden Hill, during the nineteenth century one of the city's most exclusive neighborhoods. Track-lined C Street, one block above Broadway, is also an important thoroughfare, carrying the San Diego Trolley from Santa Fe Station toward the MTS building on Imperial Avenue, and beyond, toward Tijuana.

The area south of Broadway is known as the Gaslamp Quarter, a predominantly commercial district that retains some reminders of its red-light days despite a city-backed campaign to gentrify the area. North of Broadway, the high-rises continue for a few blocks, gradually yielding to apartments and homes as the streets climb through Banker's Hill toward Hillcrest.

As you leave downtown, the land rises slowly in all

directions except to the south, where the flat coastal plain continues down to Mexico. To the north and northeast, the elevation rises gradually, drops abruptly into Mission Valley, then climbs again. Many of San Diego's best-known and oldest neighborhoods, including Mission Hills, University Heights, Talmadge, and Kensington, are built on the southern cliffs overlooking Mission Valley. Because they were originally linked to the downtown area by the lines of the San Diego Electric Railway, the neighborhoods were originally known as "streetcar suburbs." Homes on these promontories reflect the many architectural fads that have swept the city in its more recent history; Spanish colonial–revival and California-style bungalows are especially abundant. Even newer homes, like those on the bluffs in Normal Heights, recall important local history, reminding San Diegans of the devastating fire that swept up from Mission Valley in 1985, destroying hundreds of homes in its path.

East of downtown, the mesas rise toward the foothills of the Laguna Mountains, interrupted by a steep dip into El Cajon Valley about twelve miles inland. In all directions, the steady climb frequently is broken by small canyons, which add romance and charm to the city's layout and force many streets either to dead-end suddenly or to adopt winding, roundabout routes.

Downtown San Diego basically is laid out in a grid pattern. Streets running north-south are numbered (First, Second, Third). Those running east-west are alphabetical, named either after trees (Ash, Beech, Cedar) or letters. The whole system breaks down the moment it runs into a canyon or bluff, however. If you get lost, head west: You'll either find a freeway or run into the Pacific eventually.

Of course, the best way to appreciate San Diego is to get out into it. The most convenient way to do this is with a car. San Diego is well served by a number of highways

which make auto touring easy. At first glance, the Inter-
states, state Routes, surface streets, and interchanges may
seem a complicated mess. But the truth is they provide
safe, fast access to the county's far-flung treasures and are
the only way you can tackle the area's vast beauty. You're
invited to abandon the car and stroll, picnic, or hike to
your heart's content once you get where you're going.

The major north-south route in San Diego County is
Interstate 5, which passes through downtown on its way
down to Mexico and up to the beach cities of coastal
North County. Interstate 15 is the inland north-south
alternative, serving communities from Tierrasanta to Escondido and beyond, all the way to Las Vegas.

The primary east-west route in the county is Interstate
8, which originates in Ocean Beach and heads east
through El Cajon, up over the mountains and down into
the desert. State Route 94 in the south and state Route
78 in the north provide east-west access to inland communities below and above I-8. Both El Cajon Boulevard and
University Avenue serve as east-west surface-street alternatives within San Diego city limits, but because they end
in El Cajon and La Mesa respectively, their usefulness is
limited.

The most picturesque route out of downtown San
Diego is provided by the Cabrillo Freeway (state Route
163), which follows the deep canyon that cuts through
the western half of Balboa Park, then drops into Mission
Valley, where it meets up with I-8. If you travel on this
route keep your eyes peeled: In recent years, traffic on
Route 163 frequently has been brought to a precautionary
standstill as keepers from the nearby San Diego Zoo have
chased fugitive orangutans over the steep banks on the
freeway's east side. As it snakes toward the valley, Route
163 passes underneath the seven arches of the Cabrillo
Bridge, the grand entrance to Balboa Park built for the
1915 Panama-California Exposition.

After dropping into Mission Valley, Route 163 climbs into the northern neighborhoods of Linda Vista, Clairemont, and Kearny Mesa, meeting up with Interstate 805 (a north-south bypass) and I-15. Clairemont is a largely residential neighborhood, built up rapidly during the 1950s and '60s and pockmarked by the rambling squalor typical of early suburbs. Kearny Mesa is a business center, second in importance only to downtown, where prefab industrial buildings have been pressed into service as retail shops and commercial offices. Only Linda Vista, where Vietnamese restaurants and shops jostle with the Spanish-Moorish buildings of the University of San Diego, is really worth investigating.

Taken west from Route 163, I-8 cuts through a concentration of inns known as Hotel Circle, then passes north of Old Town, over I-5, and into Ocean Beach. During the late 1960s and early 1970s, Ocean Beach was a haven for local flower children and the streets in the neighborhood are still dotted with some of the funky relics of the hippie-hangout years, including the venerable O.B. People's Food Store. The main drag in Ocean Beach is Sunset Cliffs Boulevard. Taken north, over the San Diego River floodway, the road heads past Sea World into Mission Beach and Pacific Beach, two very popular coastal neighborhoods with more panache than Ocean Beach. If you go south on the boulevard, you drive toward the western side of the Point Loma peninsula and pass Sunset Cliffs Park, one of the finest surfing beaches in San Diego.

Taken east from Route 163, I-8 travels the length of Mission Valley, past La Mision de San Diego de Alcalá and San Diego State University (SDSU), down into the stunning El Cajon Valley and up into the rugged mountain areas of San Diego County. Along the way, the route passes by San Diego Jack Murphy Stadium (named for a former *San Diego Union* sports reporter, and the home of the Chargers football team and the Padres baseball club), Del Cerro (a largely Jewish neighborhood with, sad to say, only one passable delicatessen), through the incorporated cities of La Mesa and El Cajon, and into the rolling back country. Although modern subdivisions are beginning to spread into the region, generally speaking the farther east you head into the foothills, mountains, and high desert flats on I-8 the more rural and uninhabited things get. Beyond Alpine, there are small towns here and there, most of them south of I-8, but the bulk of this rugged terrain is part of the oak-, cedar-, and pine-covered Cleveland National Forest, unchanged since the days when the Kumeyaay wandered around it. The little snow that falls in San Diego comes down in the higher elevations here, and, during particularly heavy winter storms, I-8 is closed to vehicles without chains.

If you go north on the Sunrise Highway, which intersects I-8 about forty miles east of downtown just above Pine Valley, the winding road takes you through the Laguna Recreation Area, with its delightful cabins and striking desert views, past the Cuyamaca Reservoir, and into the town of Julian, famous for its annual apple festival. From here, you can either head north toward Santa Ysabel, where the Spanish missionaries established a much-needed *asistencia* in 1818, or drop down into Borrego Springs, a small but increasingly popular desert retreat surrounded by the 600,000-acre Anza-Borrego Desert State Park.

Tijuana, Mexico, lies at the southern end of Interstate 5, just fifteen miles below downtown. On the U.S. side of the border is San Ysidro, a booming, bilingual neighborhood with its share of Border Patrol agents, moneychangers, and smugglers. Though separated from downtown by the incorporated cities of Chula Vista and National City—and miles of muddy coastal plain—San Ysidro is indeed part of the city of San Diego. The area was originally settled in 1908 by the "Little Landers," a group of agricultural utopians who named the place after Saint Isadore, the patron saint of plowmen. Like most utopians, the Little Landers got nowhere fast. By 1916, their colony was gone, the victim of bad planning and the devastating floods associated with Hatfield the Rainmaker (see page 119). These days, the dun-colored mesas east of San Ysidro are dotted with companies participating in the growing *maquiladora*, or "twin-plant" program, a controversial scheme that permits American companies to ship raw materials into Mexico, where they are assembled into finished goods and then returned to the U.S. for packaging and sale. Companies taking advantage of this cross-border program—which has been condemned by American unions—pay tax only on the value added to the product in Mexico, which, given the prevailing wage in that country, isn't much. Even without factoring in the enormous amount of illegal traffic that flows across the frontier here, San Ysidro is considered the busiest border crossing in the world.

As you drive north on I-5, back toward downtown, you pass by the headquarters of the U.S. Navy's Pacific Fleet and the cities of Imperial Beach, Chula Vista, and National City. Imperial Beach is the southernmost beach in California. Unfortunately, it also happens to be the one of the most polluted beaches in the state. The problem here is the untreated sewage that the city of Tijuana releases into the Tijuana River. Because Imperial Beach lies at the mouth of this river ... well, you can smell the rest. The city is also bankrupt and depends on the Border Patrol for the little law enforcement it gets. Not a high spot, though the Tijuana Slough National Wildlife Refuge, home to a number of endangered bird species, makes a trip to Imperial Beach worthwhile, especially for bird-watchers. Just north of Imperial Beach is Coronado, a delightful little community with tree-lined streets and a clean-cut, college-town flavor. Nick Reynolds, the former

Kingston Trio member (he was the *short* one), lives in Coronado, and can occasionally be caught at Bula's, a tiny nightclub at the north end of Orange Avenue.

North from downtown, I-5 skirts the eastern limits of Mission Beach, Pacific Beach, and La Jolla. The best way to tour these communities is on San Diego's Scenic Drive, a 59-mile round-trip route that uses surface streets to cover the coastal area and many of the more significant historical spots in the city. If you take this route, clearly marked by bright blue, white, and yellow seagull signs, you can hit Black's Beach (a.k.a. Torrey Pines City Beach Park), San Diego's notorious nude beach, and then drive through La Jolla, the exclusive community poised on the bluffs and hills above the Pacific.

As I-5 continues beyond La Jolla, it passes above Sorrento Valley and enters coastal North County, one of San Diego's most important residential and recreational corridors. The sandy beaches, rugged bluffs, and marshy lagoons here help explain the enormous popularity of the surrounding communities of Del Mar, Solana Beach, Encinitas, Carlsbad, and Oceanside. During the Mexican period, North County was a series of *ranchos*, where cattle were raised to supply San Diego's growing hide and tallow trade. These days, the area is home to a string of attractive bedroom communities. Industry does thrive, however, in Leucadia, a sleepy seaside town which is the cut-flower capital of the United States, especially famous for its poinsettias. During the early spring, the hills just north of Palomar Airport Road are covered by a blanket of orange, blue, red, and yellow blooms. Hundreds of amateur and professional photographers come here each year to try to capture the magnificent sight on film.

With a dozen state and local beaches, coastal North County is also a mecca for swimmers, surfers, and sunbathers. Old Highway 101 (S21), which starts in La Jolla as Torrey Pines Road and hugs the coast as it moves north, is a good north-south alternative to I-5 if you'd like to look over the area's beaches. You can't get much closer to the Pacific without getting your feet wet.

Inland North County is a mixed bag of exclusive neighborhoods, medium-priced subdivisions (which in California means anything under $300,000), and spacious, soon-to-be-developed mesas. To the east of Del Mar is Rancho Santa Fe, the pricey preserve of some of San Diego's wealthiest citizens. The thick eucalyptus groves on the hillsides here originally were planted by the Santa Fe Railroad to provide the line with railroad ties as it expanded south. Unfortunately, eucalyptus ties were only slightly better than balsa wood ties, and the whole forest was sold to developers who platted the land into large estates. North of Rancho Santa Fe and east of Encinitas is La Costa, a glitzy inland resort community which, rumor has it, was built by the mob and bankrolled with money from the Teamsters pension fund. The Japanese own it today.

The biggest city in eastern North County is Escondido, located on the edge of San Diego's wine country and about thirty miles north of downtown on I-15. From Escondido you can visit the 1,800-acre San Diego Wild Animal Park, tour the San Pasqual Valley (site of the Battle of San Pasqual), and continue on eastward to Ramona via state Route 78, which runs through the rolling hills of the Cleveland National Forest to Santa Ysabel, Julian, and Borrego Springs.

Chapter Three
◆◆◆◆◆◆◆◆◆◆◆◆

San Diego: An A to Z Survival Guide

Alcohol

THE OFFICIAL stance on alcohol is so confusing it may drive you to drink. Liquor is available just about everywhere, *but* sales are strictly regulated. The legal drinking age is 21, *but* bars and restaurants are notorious for checking the IDs of patrons who appear to be younger than Father Time himself. State law permits the sale of alcoholic beverages between 6 A.M. and 2 A.M., *but* some stores discontinue sales much earlier. Bottles— no matter what's in them—are prohibited on all the beaches all of the time and in most parks most of the time. The consumption of alcohol is forbidden after 8 P.M. on many beaches, including Mission Beach and Pacific Beach, and prohibited twenty-four hours a day at La Jolla Shores, the boardwalk, and on all city streets. At the more popular beaches, enforcement of the booze ban is swift and certain. At parks throughout the city, it's possible—though by no means *legal*—to enjoy a beer or a glass of wine with your picnic. When in doubt, consult the posted restrictions. Driving under the influence of alcohol is illegal everywhere; punishment is harsh and very costly. If your blood alcohol content is at or above .08, you're going to jail, so imbibe sensibly, or, better yet, take a taxi.

Beaches

San Diego has fifty-five miles of coastline stretching from Oceanside to the Mexican border. Some sandy spots are better than others—depending on whether you want to surf, swim, or play with your children. For surfing, Point Loma's Sunset Cliffs (access is via a stairwell at the corner of Santa Cruz Avenue and Sunset Cliffs Boulevard), La Jolla's Windansea Beach (at the foot of Nautilus Street), and Encinitas's Swami's Surfing Park (just below the Self-Realization Fellowship) are highly recommended. For swimming, the beach in front of Coronado's Hotel del Coronado, the waters off La Jolla's Black's Beach, and both Mission Bay and Mission Beach are probably best. Families with children are advised to use La Jolla's Children's Cove or the many miles of sand beside the placid waters of Mission Bay.

If you venture down to the beach in Mexico, use extreme caution and wear shoes. There are few lifeguards south of the border and, because the sand is not maintained as it is in San Diego, there are broken bottles and jagged-edged hazards everywhere. Remember, too, to wear shoes with thick, nonskid soles when you explore San Diego's many tidepools. For more information on beach safety, see "Rip Tides" below.

Churches

San Diego was settled by Catholics, but virtually every religious persuasion has adherents here now—including several New Age groups. What follows is an overview of local houses of worship. Service times were current at press time. The area code for all telephone numbers is 619.

Assemblies of God: Assembly of God, 2069 Ebers Street, Ocean Beach (224-5359).

Baptist: First Baptist Church of Coronado, 445 C Street, Coronado (435-6588). Sunday school at 9 A.M., worship at 10 A.M., Sunday.

Catholic: St. Joseph's Cathedral, 1535 Third Avenue, downtown (238-0229). The Tridentine Latin Mass, banned by Vatican II but making a comeback in some dioceses, is celebrated every Sunday at 9 A.M. in the mausoleum at Holy Cross Cemetery. On the last Sunday of the month, Gregorian chants are sung as well.

Congregationalist: Congregational Church of La Jolla, 1216 Cave Street, La Jolla (459-5045). Services at 10 A.M., Sunday.

Disciples of Christ: Pacific Beach Christian Church, 1074 Loring Street, Pacific Beach (483-4504). Worship at 8 and 10 A.M., Sunday.

Drive-In: Chula Vista Community Church, 3265 National City Boulevard, National City (422-7850). Sunday, 9 A.M. Only in California!

Eastern Orthodox: St. Spyridon Greek Orthodox Church, 3655 Park Boulevard (297-4165). Holy Liturgy 10 A.M., Sunday. Weekday and holiday services at 9 A.M.

Episcopalian: St. Paul's Cathedral, 2728 Sixth Avenue, downtown (298-7261). Holy Eucharist at 8 and 10:30 A.M., Sunday. Evensong (September through May) 5 P.M., Sunday.

Evangelical: Puritan Evangelical Church of America, 6374 Potomac Street, Paradise Hills (479-5053). Services are held at 11 A.M. and 6:30 P.M., Sunday.

Islamic: Masjidul Taqwa Mosque, 2575 Imperial Avenue, San Diego (239-6738).

Jehovah's Witness: Jehovah's Witness, Hillcrest Congregation, 2035 Adams Avenue, North Park (295-2300).

Jewish (Conservative): Tifereth Israel, 6660 Cowles Mountain Boulevard, Del Cerro (697-6001). Erev Shabbat 8 P.M., Friday. Shabbat and Yom Tov 9:15 A.M., Saturday. *Jewish (Orthodox)*: Beth Jacob, 4855 College Avenue, Del Cerro (287-9890). Sabbath services at sunset Friday. Saturday services at 7:45 and 8:45 A.M. *Jewish (Reform)*: Beth Israel, 2512 Third Avenue, downtown (239-0149). Friday, 8:15 P.M.

Lutheran: First Lutheran Church, 1420 Third Avenue, downtown (234-6149). Traditional Liturgical 9 A.M., Sunday. Contemporary 11 A.M., Sunday.

Methodist: Park Boulevard United Methodist Church, 4075 Park Boulevard, uptown (295-0687). Services at 11 A.M., Sunday.

Mormon: San Diego First Ward Stake Hall, 4005 Hamilton Street, North Park (298-2492). Sacramental service 12:30 P.M., Sunday.

New Age: There is a Self-Realization Fellowship Church in Hillcrest at 3068 First Avenue (295-0170), but the gold-spired mother of all temples, built by Paramahansa Yogananda himself, is located in Encinitas at 215 K Street (753-2888). The Hare Krishnas operate a temple and visitor center at 1030 Grand Avenue, Pacific Beach (483-2500).

Presbyterian: Pacific Beach Presbyterian, 1675 Garnet Avenue (273-9312). Services at 8 and 10 A.M., Sunday.

Southern Baptist: Calvary Southern Baptist Church, 6866 Linda Vista Road, Linda Vista (277-7078). Worship at 11 A.M. and 6 P.M., Sunday.

Unitarian: First Unitarian Church, 4190 Front Street, Hillcrest (298-9978).

Clothing and Climate

San Diego enjoys over 3,200 hours of sunshine each year (about seventy-five percent of the maximum possible) and an average daily temperature in the high 60s, so you'll be comfortable in summer clothing most months of the year. Still, the thermometer can drop, especially on winter nights, so you're advised to pack a sweater or windbreaker. Good-looking casual wear is *de rigueur*, but sartorial standards are otherwise fairly laid-back. Keep your dinner jacket or evening wear at home unless you're attending a formal event or interested in one of the few dining spots that require a coat and tie (see Chapter 9).

The ten inches of precipitation the city gets each year normally fall between October and April. Although drenching tropical storms occasionally hit the city, rainstorms are usually brief and followed by sunny skies, so you can do without an umbrella if you're willing to sit out the short showers. Cool waters offshore cause early-morning and late-evening fogs, especially during the winter months, but these usually "burn off" by mid-morning. The warmest days come during the late summer and early fall, when hot, dry winds called "Santa Anas" periodically blow in from the desert, clearing the eastern skies of any dust or smog, driving temperatures into the high 90s and low 100s, and creating spectacular sunsets. The condition rarely lasts longer than three or four days.

Earthquakes

O.K., they happen, but they can be fun—provided you take precautions. And once you've experienced a temblor you automatically become an honorary Californian. If you have an exaggerated fear of seismic activity, you'll probably find little comfort in the fact that downtown San Diego is built over something called the Rose Canyon

Fault. Fortunately, most of the earthquakes that shake the county have epicenters hundreds of miles away and pass unnoticed. The last significant earthquake to jar San Diego hit in 1862.

Still, scientists predict that within the next thirty years San Diego has a sixty percent chance of having an earthquake with a magnitude of 7.0 or greater on the Richter scale, so preparedness is important. There is an enormous amount of folklore and superstition surrounding tremors, including the mistaken belief that they are preceded by close, gray, muggy conditions known as "earthquake weather." Here are the facts. The first and perhaps most important thing to realize is that earthquakes don't kill people; falling objects, flying glass, and ruptured gas lines do. If you're indoors when an earthquake strikes, stay there. Move away from windows, bookcases, cupboards, and appliances. Do not go outside. DUCK under the nearest desk, table, or chair and HOLD on to it. If you can't find suitable cover quickly, stand underneath the nearest doorway and remain there until the shaking stops. If you're outside when the earthquake hits, move into an open space, away from buildings and power lines, drop to the ground, and cover your head. Once the tremors stop, don't smoke or light candles until you're sure there are no potentially explosive gas leaks. For recorded information about earthquake preparedness, call the city's earthquake-disaster information line at 234-3128. And relax: Although long-term residents shouldn't downplay the potential dangers associated with earthquakes, visitors are better advised to worry about other natural threats, including rip tides (see below).

Foreign Currency

Although a number of local banks have currency exchange departments in their bigger offices, their rates are nothing short of usurious. If you're looking to buy or unload Deutschmarks, Francs, or Canadian dollars, your best bet is Thomas Cook Foreign Exchange at Horton Plaza in downtown (235-0900) or at University Towne Center in La Jolla (457-0841), or the American Express Travel Service office at 1020 Prospect Street in La Jolla (459-4161). Both also accept wire transfers. If you're heading to Mexico, don't be lured by the moneychangers in San Ysidro. Dollars are gratefully accepted in Tijuana and pesos only get in the way of hardball haggling.

Hospitals

San Diego is well stocked in this department. Given the city's booming biomedical industry, it's only natural that there are also some world-class medical centers as well. Mercy Hospital (4077 Fifth Avenue, Hillcrest) is the city's oldest, established by the Sisters of Mercy in 1889. Many prominent locals have been delivered here over the years. The UCSD Medical Center (22 Dickson Street, Hillcrest) operates in association with the UCSD School of Medicine. Also good are Green Hospital of Scripps Clinic (overlooking the Torrey Pines Municipal Golf Course at 1066 N. Torrey Pines Road, La Jolla), Children's Hospital (8001 Frost Street, Linda Vista) and Grossmont Hospital (5555 Grossmont Center Drive, La Mesa).

Jaywalking

You may consider it quaint, you may consider it absurd, but consider this: The San Diego Police Department aggressively enforces the law against jaywalking. There are no warnings and the fine is $20 for the first offense. Cross only at intersections or clearly marked crosswalks. If the pedestrian sign is flashing "Don't Walk," *don't*.

Los Angeles

With one foot in the ocean, one foot in the desert, and its back to Mexico, San Diego faces north, toward . . . Los Angeles. For some San Diegans, this forced familiarity with LA has bred contempt. They demonize every aspect of our northern neighbor (which they derisively refer to as "Smell-A") and define themselves largely in *opposition* to their Angelino cousins. Other San Diegans can't get enough of the place. They go ga-ga over every half-baked LA fad and condemn San Diego precisely because it isn't more like Los Angeles. The point here is that San Diegans are the last people you should turn to for unbiased information about Los Angeles. The only thing we can agree on is how to get there—or how to avoid it. To get to Los Angeles from San Diego, take Interstate 5 north about 120 miles. To get to Hollywood, take state Route 101 north off I-5, get off at Sunset or Hollywood Boulevard, and head west.

Top nightspots in the area include the Formosa Cafe at 7156 Santa Monica Boulevard (213-850-9050), Yamashiro's at 199 N. Sycamore Avenue (213-466-5125), Nicko Dell at 5511 Melrose Avenue (213-469-2181), and Geoffrey's at 27400 Pacific Coast Highway in Malibu (310-457-1519). The Formosa is a garrulous Chinese restaurant and bar, favored by up-and-coming actors and Hollywood hangers-on. Both Molly Ringwald and Tim Robbins have been spotted there recently. Yamashiro's, nestled in the Hollywood Hills, is more sedate but its views of Los Angeles are something to shout about. Geoffrey's, in super-exclusive Malibu, overlooks Santa Monica Bay. The table to request here is the Crow's Nest—a cozy two-top on the roof that offers stunning views of Catalina Island and endless romantic possibilities.

Whatever you do, don't step foot into Musso & Frank's on Hollywood Boulevard. It has become a tourist trap of the worst kind, with abominable food, objectionable service, and outrageous prices. You can eat at Wolfgang Puck's Spago for the same price.

If you have time, consider a jaunt down Wilshire Boulevard to catch some of Southern California's best Art Moderne architecture or a stroll down Melrose Avenue, where you'll catch a glimpse of LA at its trendiest. Consider a visit to the world-famous Bradbury Building at 304 S. Broadway in downtown LA, with its wrought-iron metalwork and stunning lighting. Tours of the Bradbury, one of only four buildings in the entire LA area that have made it onto the National Register of Historic Places, are by appointment only. Call 213-626-1893 for information.

Mexico

Mexico begins just fifteen miles south of downtown San Diego, making a cross-border jaunt into Tijuana, Tecate, or any of the cities at the northern tip of the Baja peninsula convenient and easy. When you go—and, really, you should—remember this: Mexico still operates under the Napoleonic Code. Criminals aren't coddled down here, and, unfortunately, neither are suspects. There is no presumption of innocence, no Fourth Amendment—none of the procedural safeguards from official harassment or intimidation with which we're familiar. So behave yourself.

An important note about driving down in Baja: Because your U.S. auto insurance isn't valid in Mexico, even minor traffic accidents can turn into major trip-ruining incidents. If you're involved in a fender bender and you don't have Mexican insurance, *Adios amigo*: You've just committed a felony under Mexican law and you'll be detained in a Mexican jail. (It *sounds* bad, but it's actually much worse.) You won't be released until you pay all the fines and damages arising from the accident. If you're motoring outside the northern limits of Baja, the rules are even more stringent. You will need an original copy of your auto insurance policy (photocopies are unacceptable) *and* Mexican insurance, valid for a minimum of two months from the date of entry. If there's a lien on your title, you're also going to need a letter from the lien-holder giving you permission to bring the vehicle into Mexico. If you forget these documents, you'll be required to post a cash bond of one-hundred percent of the value of your vehicle, as assessed by cranky, underpaid guards who have little idea how much your car is really worth. Note also that most rental-car companies expressly forbid renters from taking the cars into Mexico. Check *before* crossing the border.

A final driving advisory: Though Mexican officials are busy creating a mail-in payment system for traffic fines, for now the old system is still being followed. If you're stopped by a Mexican policeman for a traffic violation— and the chances are good that you will be—the officer will ask you to follow him to the nearest police station, where you'll pay the fine and get your receipt.

If all this makes driving in Mexico sound like less than great fun, there are a number of companies in San Diego licensed to issue Mexican insurance policies. The coverage normally costs about $12 per day. Otherwise, park your car in downtown San Diego, jump on the trolley to San Ysidro (the fare is $1.50 for adults and kids; 60 cents for seniors), walk across the border, and hop into one of the many cabs queuing on the other side. The ride to Avenida Revolución, the main drag in Tijuana, should run you about $5.

Returning to the United States, visitors are permitted to bring back $400 worth of non-Mexican imports, tax-free. Foreign-made goods above the $400 limit are taxed at 10 percent. And because Mexico qualifies as a developing country under the General System of Preferences,

U.S. visitors may return with an almost unlimited amount of Mexican-made curios and curiosities without paying any tariff. If you're over 21 years of age, the good news is you're permitted to bring one liter of booze back into the U.S., duty-free. The bad news? Much of the liquor sold down here is not worth the effort of lugging it back over the border.

As long as you behave yourself and avoid getting behind the wheel of your car, your visit to Mexico should be trouble-free. Although Mexico is a foreign country, its laws are not entirely alien and most problems can be avoided if you use common sense. Possession of illegal drugs is, for instance, as illegal down here as it is back in the United States, and offenders face long imprisonment if caught. Drinking in public is also forbidden. If you find yourself in a pickle, contact the Tijuana Tourist Protection Bureau at 81-94-94 or the American Consulate at 81-74-00.

Museums

San Diego has a number of worthwhile cultural attractions including, of course, Balboa Park, which is home to the largest concentration of museums outside Washington, D.C. Here is an overview of the more popular spots:

California Surf Museum: Features permanent and revolving exhibits concerning the history and development of surfing. 308 N. Pacific Street, Oceanside; 619-721-6876. Open Saturday and Sunday only.

Centro Cultural: A museum/theater complex in Tijuana that screens "People of the Sun," a ninety-minute travelogue on Mexico, in its Omnimax theater every afternoon at 2. Paseo de los Heroes and Mina, Tijuana; 706-684-1132. Open daily from 10 to 5.

Mingei International Museum of Folk Art: Exhibits

permanent and revolving collections of folk and ceremonial art from around the world. 4405 La Jolla Village Drive, inside University Towne Center shopping mall; 453-5300. Open daily from 10 to 5.

Museum of Photographic Arts: Exhibits permanent and visiting exhibits by contemporary photographers. Balboa Park; 619-239-5262. Open daily from 9 to 5; Thursdays till 9.

Museum of San Diego History: Hosts traveling and permanent hands-on exhibits exploring the local impact of national history.

Balboa Park; 619-232-6203. Open Wednesday through Sunday from 10 to 4.

Natural History Museum: Features permanent and temporary exhibits concerning man and his environment. Balboa Park; phone 232-3821. Open daily from 10 to 4; Thursdays till 9.

Reuben H. Fleet Space Theater and Science Center: A hands-on classroom with an Omnimax theater showing stunning documentaries and novelty laser shows set to rock music. Balboa Park; 619-238-1168. Open daily from 9:30 to 9; Fridays and Saturdays till 10:30.

San Diego Aerospace Museum: Features permanent exhibits of aircraft, scale models, and aviation-related items from the days of hot-air balloons to the present. Balboa Park; 619-234-8291. Open daily from 10 to 4.

San Diego Automotive Museum: Exhibits permanent and revolving collections of vintage automobiles. Balboa Park; phone 231-2886. Open daily from 10 to 4.

San Diego Hall of Champions: Exhibits a permanent collection of memorabilia from the world of professional sports. Balboa Park; 234-2544. Open daily from 10 to 4.

San Diego Maritime Museum: Three historic vessels exhibit displays exploring local and regional maritime history. The Embarcadero at Harbor Drive and Ash Street; 619-234-9153. Open daily from 9 to 8.

San Diego Museum of Art: Houses a permanent collection of paintings, from Renaissance portraiture to the most modern abstraction. An outdoor sculpture garden and café add to the museum's appeal. Balboa Park; 232-7931. Open daily from 10 to 4.

San Diego Museum of Contemporary Art: Displays permanent and traveling exhibits of modern and postmodern art. 700 Prospect Street, La Jolla; 454-3541. Open daily from 10 to 5; Sunday and Wednesday till 9.

San Diego Museum of Man: Features permanent and traveling exhibits exploring modern man's ancestors. Balboa Park; 619-239-2001. Open daily from 10 to 4.

Serra Museum: Displays artifacts from San Diego's Hispanic period. Presidio Park, just above Old Town; 297-3258.

Newspapers and Magazines

Although the demise of the *San Diego Tribune* in early 1992 robbed the city of its only Pulitzer Prize—winning newspaper, San Diego still has two daily papers. The *San Diego Union-Tribune* (formerly the *Union*) provides good local, national, and international coverage, dependable music and theater reviews, and advance notice of upcoming weekend events. The *San Diego Daily Transcript* covers the city's business beat, five days a week, and is a solid source for local real-estate and biotech news. In addition to the dailies, there are a host of lively periodicals covering the city, including *San Diego Magazine*, one of the nation's first city magazines and still one of the best, and the *Reader*, a free weekly crammed with exposés and attack journalism, which offers the most comprehensive and up-to-date events listings for San Diego. It comes out on Thursdays.

Parking

Although it isn't a problem in most sections of the city, parking can be extremely tight in downtown, Hillcrest, and the beach areas. Metered on-street parking is available in these neighborhoods, but scarce. If you opt for a meter, feed it and obey all posted restrictions—enforcement borders on the obsessive here. Garages and lots are numerous and their charges vary widely depending on the time of day and any events that may be taking place nearby. Better restaurants in neighborhoods where parking is tough usually offer free or low-cost valet service.

Phone Numbers

The area code for all numbers is 619.

Police or Fire: 911
American Youth Hostel: 239-2644
Beach and Surf Report: 221-8884
Beach Parks and Recreation: 221-8900
California Bar Association Legal Line (free preliminary advice): 231-8585
City-sponsored activities in Balboa Park: 525-8209
Convention and Visitors Bureau: 232-3101
Crime Victims' Assistance: 236-0101
International Visitors Information: 236-1212
Municipal Golf Courses: 232-2470 or 453-0380
Non-emergency health questions (free call): 696-8100
Poison Center: 543-6000
Transit queries: 233-3004
Travelers Aid: 232-7991
U.S. Forest Service (for information on Mt. Laguna and Cleveland National Forest): 473-8547
Weather Report (24-hour): 289-1212

Post Offices

The U.S. Postal Service has stations throughout San Diego, including a massive main office at 2535 Midway Drive (574-0477) and two convenient beach satellites at 4640 Cass Street in Pacific Beach (272-6545) and 1140 Wall Street in La Jolla (454-7139). In downtown, stop by the old main post office at 815 E Street (232-5096), one of the many buildings the Works Progress Administration (WPA) erected in San Diego during the Depression and a fine example of Art Deco design.

Rip Tides

Rip tides are powerful currents that snatch hapless swimmers out of the safe, shallow waters close to shore and drag them out to sea. Especially common during the winter, when currents generated by violent storms tear away at the ocean floor and create treacherous undertows, rip tides can occur anywhere at any time. Swimmers can avoid catastrophe, however, by following a few basic precautions. First, swim only at beaches where lifeguards are on duty and *pay attention* to what they tell you. Lifeguards have a keen eye for rip tides and other unseen hazards and will advise beachgoers about what is safe and what isn't, but it's really up to you to listen. Second, treat empty waters and deserted beaches the way you'd treat a dark alley in an unfamiliar neighborhood. There's probably a reason why no one is there.

If you find yourself in a rip tide, remain calm. Do not fight the current by attempting to swim directly to shore. That is a battle dozens of distressed swimmers fight every year . . . and lose. Instead, swim parallel to the shore, for about twenty-five to fifty yards (most rips are very narrow and this should get you out of its pull), and then try again to make your way back in. If you're still in trouble, remain calm. Signal to the lifeguard, then resume your course parallel to the shore. Help probably will be on the way already. A good way to avoid problems is to buy yourself a pair of swim fins, equipment even the lifeguards consider essential.

Sales Tax

You'll pay 7.75 percent on purchases and 9 percent on hotel bills. If it makes you feel any better, one dollar of every nine raised by the hotel-motel tax is used to fund improvements in Balboa Park and Mission Bay.

Spectator Sports

San Diego's professional baseball, football, soccer, and hockey teams are a source of year-round entertainment for natives and newcomers alike. *Baseball*: San Diego Padres, April through October, San Diego Jack Murphy Stadium. Ticket prices range from $5 to $11. Call 283-7294 for more information. *Football*: San Diego Chargers, September through December, San Diego Jack Murphy Stadium. Ticket prices range from $18 to $30. Call 563-8281 for more information. *Indoor Soccer*: San Diego Sockers, October through April, San Diego Sports Arena. Ticket prices range from $8 to $16. Call 224-4625 for more information. *Hockey*: San Diego Gulls, October through April, San Diego Sports Arena. Ticket prices range from $7 to $16. Call 225-7825 for more information.

Taxis

Unless you're at the airport, the train station, or a major hotel, it's almost impossible to hail a cab in San Diego, so phone ahead. Numbers are listed in the telephone directory. If you can, use La Jolla or Coronado cab companies, which provide extra-clean cars and very courteous drivers. The airport is also served by a number of shuttle companies, including SuperShuttle and Coast Shuttle, but these are more costly. Taxi fares run from $1 to $1.60 for the first eighth of a mile and from $1.20 to $1.80 for every mile thereafter. There is no extra charge for extra passengers.

Transit System

The Metropolitan Transit System (MTS) serves the San Diego area, from La Jolla to the Mexican border, with regularly scheduled buses, trolleys, and vans. It can't compare with the mass-transit systems in San Francisco or London, but it does a reasonably good job given the vast area it's required to cover, particularly if you're beginning or ending your trip in the downtown area. One-way bus fares run from $1 to $2. The onboard fareboxes take dollar bills but do not dispense change. Trolley fares range from 50 cents to $2 and tickets must be purchased before you get on. For information about fares and schedules, phone 233-3004 between 5:30 A.M. and 8:30 P.M. If you're downtown, stop by the Transit Store at the corner of Fifth Avenue and Broadway for maps, schedules, and money-saving discount books good for travel on the trolley and buses.

Dial-a-Ride, which provides door-to-door service for just $1, is available to everyone in La Mesa, Lemon Grove, and El Cajon and to the handicapped and seniors in San Diego. The MTS also serves the back country, though infrequently. For information on southeast rural routes (Alpine, Campo, Descanso, Jacumba, or Jamul), call 478-5875. For desert and northeast rural routes (Ramona, Santa Ysabel, Warner Springs, Julian, or Borrego Springs), call 765-0145.

If you're just interested in getting your bearings, consider Molley Trolleys. These privately-run sightseeing buses, modified to look like old-fashioned railway cars, provide two-hour mini-tours of San Diego and will pick you up and drop you off at your hotel, all for around $5. For more information, call 233-9177.

Zoos

The San Diego Zoo, located off Park Boulevard in Balboa Park, is one of the city's most popular attractions for visitors and locals alike. The cage-free exhibits here house one of the best and most famous collections of wild and endangered species in the world, including koalas, lions, bears, giraffes, snakes, gorillas, and birds of all feathers.

The zoo is open from 9 to 4 seven days a week. Admission is $12 for adults and $4 for children ages 3 through 15. Parking in the lot on Park Avenue is free. Phone 234-3153 for more information.

The San Diego Wild Animal Park, located about thirty miles north of downtown San Diego in Escondido, is an 1,800-acre wildlife preserve where animals from Asia and Africa roam in semifreedom. Midsummer weather can get rather hot and stuffy out here, so visitors are advised to dress appropriately.

The Wild Animal Park is open daily from 9 to 4. Admission is $16 for adults and $9 for children ages 3 through 15. Phone 234-6541 for information.

PART TWO
♦♦♦♦♦♦♦♦♦

EXPLORING
SAN DIEGO

Chapter Four
◆◆◆◆◆◆◆◆◆◆◆

Exploring Downtown

S AN DIEGO'S modern era began in 1867, when
Alonzo Horton bought a thousand acres of chaparral-covered land south of Old Town and transformed it
almost overnight into a 226-block subdivision called New
Town. Although chronic bouts of real-estate fever kept
it off balance during the early years, San Diego's new
downtown stabilized and grew, becoming the principal
commercial and residential quarter in the city and relegat-
ing Old Town to the history books in very short order.

Horton's original development was confined to the
southern edge of present-day downtown, below Market
Street. But as the excitement and speculation over New
Town built during the 1870s and '80s, the district expanded in all directions. Although the area stagnated between 1930 and 1970, as suburban shopping malls
siphoned off customers, a two-decade revitalization effort
has reclaimed downtown San Diego. Today, it is once
again the city's center, drawing visitors and locals alike
with its bustling commercial district, restaurants, and
nightlife.

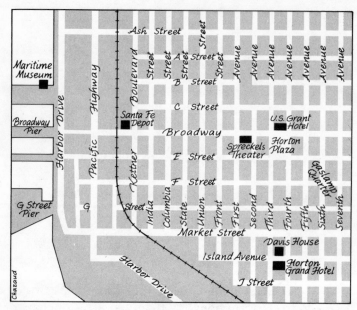

Downtown San Diego

Because downtown was established well after the Spanish and Mexican periods ended, modern-day visitors will find no reminders of San Diego's rich Hispanic history here. But the district, nevertheless, is full of relics from the city's wild American years and well worth a visit.

One of the city's wildest periods came during the early decades of the twentieth century, when many downtown residents moved into the outlying neighborhoods of Mission Hills, East San Diego, and North Park, far removed from the inner city. Stripped of its respectable citizenry by this population shift, downtown became a bawdy playpen for pleasure-seekers. These were the days of the sprawling Stingaree, San Diego's notorious red-light district, with its bars, opium dens, brothels, and gambling houses. These were also the days of Ida Bailey, the city's most famous madam and the self-proclaimed Queen of the Stingaree. Bailey's lemon-colored cathouse on Fourth Avenue, nicknamed the "Canary Cottage," was a home-away-from-home for many of the city's most prominent citizens, who visited the fleshy den with one eye on carnal pleasure and the other on the nearest exit. Not surprisingly, raids on the neighborhood were common. During one sweep of the Stingaree in 1912, the San Diego Police Department nabbed over a hundred and fifty prostitutes. When the police chief gave the unfortunate women the opportunity to leave town rather than pay the $100 fine, many took advantage of the offer—and the chief—by buying round-trip tickets to nearby Los Angeles.

As the U.S. Navy increased its presence in San Diego during the 1920s and '30s, the Stingaree grew, attracting sailors, stevedores and dockworkers with its pawnshops, shooting galleries, and bars. Even Prohibition couldn't stop the flow of booze in the Stingaree, where, thanks to the rum-running boats that sped between Ensenada in Mexico and San Diego, the speakeasies operated as if the Eighteenth Amendment had never passed. With the lifting of Prohibition in December 1933, the area languished, as adult theaters, hostess bars, and sex-aid shops moved into the neighborhood and the swabbies moved to West Broadway. Recently, the Stingaree has been reborn as the Gaslamp Quarter, a 16-block National Historic District, which boasts some of the hottest nightclubs and trendiest restaurants in the city. A few reminders of the neighborhood's gaudy past remain, including Ida Bailey's Restaurant in the Horton Grand Hotel, built on the site of the infamous yellow bordello.

The Embarcadero

Alonzo Horton's New Town gamble paid off thanks to the growth of the shipping and tuna industries and the development of a permanent U.S. Navy presence in the city. Perched on the edge of San Diego's increasingly important harbor, New Town and the subdivisions that followed were perfectly placed to exploit the city's maritime trade. Although very few visitors arrive by boat these days, the embarcadero, or waterfront, is nevertheless a good place to begin exploring downtown San Diego.

Start at the western end of Broadway, just north of the 11th Naval District Headquarters and the Naval Supply Center, at Broadway Pier on Harbor Drive. During the 1920s and '30s, Broadway Pier housed the offices of numerous steamship companies, the California Fish and Game Service, and the Tuna Fishermen's Union. A recent $8 million facelift has made it prettier to look at, but the bustle of the old pier and surrounding wharves and warehouses is strangely absent. On weekends, Navy ships dock at the pier and offer free guided tours. Call 235-3534 for information on the events.

A few steps north of the Cruise Ship Pier, where *The Love Boat* periodically docks, are three ships belonging to the San Diego Maritime Museum: the *Star of India*, the *Berkeley*, and the *Medea*. Ironically, none of these vessels played any role whatsoever in San Diego's history. The *Star of India*—originally christened *Euterpe*—ferried immigrants from England to New Zealand and Australia during the latter half of the nineteenth century. Three recent voyages inside the harbor have proved that the vessel is still seaworthy, making it the oldest full-rigged iron ship still afloat. The *Berkeley* operated as a ferryboat between San Francisco and Oakland from 1900 to 1958. This monotonous routine was broken once, in 1906, when the *Berkeley* rescued survivors of the disastrous San

Francisco earthquake and sheered into history. The third ship, the *Medea*, was a private steam yacht, owned over the years by a number of would-be sailors, including two members of the British Parliament. The vessels, which feature onboard displays chronicling San Diego's maritime history, are open from 9 A.M. to 8 P.M., seven days a week. Admission is $5 for adults, $4 for seniors and teenagers, and $1.25 for kids.

Just north of the Maritime Museum, you may see tuna-boat crews mending their nets and taking on provisions, a relatively rare sight these days. During the tuna fleet's heyday during the 1940s and '50s, dozens of tuna boats, or seiners, sailed from "Tuna Harbor" at the G Street Pier, which was known in those days as Fisherman's Wharf. Today, the G Street Pier is home to the American Tuna Boat Association, a trade association whose clout and membership have diminished as foreign competition, cannery closings, and changing consumption patterns have weakened the American tuna industry.

Across Harbor Drive from the Maritime Museum is the San Diego County Administration Building, a well-preserved and delightfully eclectic Art Deco/Spanish Revival building erected in 1938 by the WPA. Originally, the building served as San Diego's City Hall, but when city offices moved to their present location at 202 C Street an 1964, county offices moved in. The *Guardian of Water* statue on the western side of the building, which celebrates San Diego's dedication to water conservation, was carved by Donal Hord from granite found in Lakeside. The surrounding garden is an example of the drought-tolerant, low-maintenance landscaping (or xeriscaping as it is called) necessary in the arid Southwest. President Franklin D. Roosevelt was on hand in 1938 when the building was opened with great ceremony and his son, James Roosevelt, visited to help celebrate the building's fiftieth anniversary several years ago.

A few blocks south of the County Administration Building, at the corner of Harbor Drive and Broadway, is the former site of Lane Field, where the San Diego Padres won their first Pacific Coast League pennant in 1937. The park was named for Bill Lane, the owner of the club, who brought the Padres (formerly the Hollywood Stars) down to San Diego in 1936, with future hall-of-famer and native San Diegan Ted Williams in the lineup. Lane Field was torn down in 1958, when the Padres moved to Westgate Park in Mission Valley, but some San Diegans fondly remember the days when they could take in the action at the ballpark and enjoy an unparalleled view of the harbor at the same time.

For a better view of San Diego's skyline and embarcadero, consider hopping aboard one of the many harbor cruises which depart from the area between Broadway Pier and the Cruise Ship Terminal. The one- and two-hour narrated excursions cover most points of interest on the water, including the Naval Station and North Island Naval Air Station. If you're in the city between December and February and want to see the migration of the California gray whales, you should know that whale-watching ships also depart from here.

Although regular cross-bay ferry service ceased shortly after the San Diego–Coronado Bay Bridge opened in 1969, passenger ferries have made a comeback lately and provide a cheap alternative to the conventional harbor cruise. Round-trip tickets for the fifteen-minute crossing from San Diego to the Old Ferry Landing in Coronado are $4. Bicycles are permitted onboard the ships but there is a $1 surcharge each way. Once you get to Coronado, check out the Hotel del Coronado (1500 Orange Avenue). Built in 1888, this sprawling redwood resort has been featured in many films, including *Some Like It Hot*, starring Marilyn Monroe and Jack Lemmon, and *Loving Couples*, with Susan Sarandon, James Coburn, and Shirley MacLaine. Designed by Stanford White, a noted New York architect, the Del once was the largest hotel in the world. While that title has been usurped, the Del remains the largest all-wooden structure on the West Coast and one of the most romantic hostelries anywhere. Legend has it King Edward VIII met Wallis Simpson here during the 1920s while he was still the Prince of Wales. (See Chapter 6 for more information on Coronado.)

Another way to view downtown is by strolling down the Waterfront Boardwalk, a bayside pathway that roughly parallels Harbor Drive, from Harbor Island to the Convention Center. Along the way, the boardwalk passes by Seaport Village (a commercial shopping area similar to San Francisco's Pier 39, with an ambience that is more New England than San Diego), the G Street Pier (formerly Tuna Harbor or Fisherman's Wharf), and the old San Diego Rowing Club, which is now operated as a restaurant by Chart House.

West Broadway

A few blocks east of the waterfront on Broadway is the Santa Fe Depot, a Spanish colonial-style monument to America's railway years and a deserved entry in the National Register of Historic Places. Built in 1915, in anticipation of the Panama-California Exposition, the depot was designed to conform with the architectural motifs of the fair. For many years afterward, it remained the primary arrival point for most visitors to San Diego. A much-needed renovation in the late 1970s brought back much of the gilded glamour of the depot. Visitors today are encouraged to stroll through the waiting area and admire the solid oak benches, brick floors, and magnificently high ceilings.

Across the street from the depot is a Spanish-style transformer building owned and operated by San Diego Gas

& Electric. Originally, this was the site of *Los Baños* (Span., The Baths), one of San Diego's many bathhouses, which served the city for the first thirty years of the present century. Back then, bay water was brought in to cool condensers at the nearby power plant of the San Diego Electric Railway Company; once heated, the water was piped into Los Baños, providing it with a plentiful supply of hot water and making it the most popular bathhouse and plunge on the waterfront.

During the 1950s and '60s, the West Broadway area was a slightly garish Fun Zone for underage navy enlisted men on liberty. The tattoo parlors, arcades, and strip clubs gave way in the 1980s to the shiny banks and hotels you see today, a booming economy and easy credit having turned the area into an upscale Fun Zone for loan officers, building contractors, and real-estate developers. When the ride ended in the late 1980s, one of the victims was Great American Savings and Loan, at one time San Diego's most generous corporate citizen. Freewheeling executives of Great American had planned to move into their magnificent new offices across the street from the Santa Fe Depot, but real-estate dealings in Arizona caught up with the savings and loan, and the regulators moved in first.

Farther east on Broadway is the U.S. Grant Hotel, opposite Horton Plaza. Built as a memorial to General (and President) Ulysses S. Grant by his son, Ulysses S. Grant, Jr., the $2-million hotel opened in 1910 with 426 rooms, two indoor swimming pools, and a garden roof. Presidential visitors were never in short supply here, but the Grant is perhaps most famous for the women who visited and left their mark on the hotel.

In January 1931 Alma Rubens, the star of such films as *The Price She Paid*, *The Half Breed*, and *Showboat*, was arrested at the U.S. Grant, charged with possession of forty cubes of morphine. The drugs, sewn into the hems of garments, apparently had been smuggled into the U.S. by Rubens when she returned from a trip to the Agua Caliente racetrack in Tijuana. Released by the San Diego authorities on her own recognizance, the unfortunate Rubens died two weeks later in Hollywood of a heroin overdose.

Until the 1960s, the Grant Grill, the clubby restaurant on the hotel's first floor, was an exclusively masculine enclave, off-limits to women before dinner. But in 1969 seven local ladies challenged the restriction, staging a sit-in at the Grill. After some legal wrangling and a lot of bad press, the all-male rule was scrapped and women were welcomed into the hotel's ornate inner sanctum at lunchtime. In a magnanimous gesture, given the legal costs they had incurred, the owners honored the seven women with a plaque in the restaurant. Although the hotel underwent a $60-million renovation during the mid-1980s, the architectural character of the place has been preserved and you're encouraged to take a look around the restored lobby and function rooms.

Across the street from the U.S. Grant is Horton Plaza, a fanciful shopping center sprawled out over seven blocks (see Chapter 11). In the foreground is the original Horton Plaza, a small park built by Alonzo Horton during the 1870s which he donated to the city. The fountain centerpiece was a private gift from Mayor Louis Wilde. It was dedicated on October 15, 1910, to coincide with the opening of the U.S. Grant, and was one of the first fountains to combine flowing water and colored lights. The medallions on the base honor Juan Cabrillo, Junípero Serra, and Alonzo Horton.

The Gaslamp Quarter and Environs

The Gaslamp Quarter begins just east of Horton Plaza, at the corner of Broadway and Fifth Avenue. During the

1870s, this was the business and residential center of Horton's New Town, and the board sidewalks and dusty streets were filled with the tradesmen, speculators, Indians, and outlaws who flocked to the growing city to get in on the action. As New Town spread northward during the booms of the 1880s, Fifth Avenue served as its main artery, which accounts for the high concentration of curious historical buildings here, including the Backesto Block, the Keating Building, the Nesmith-Greeley Building, and the St. James Hotel—San Diego's first high-rise.

The oldest surviving structure in the area appears to be the William Heath Davis house at the corner of Fourth and Island Avenues. In the 1850s, a full decade and a half before Alonzo Horton arrived on the scene, William Heath Davis had attempted to create a new San Diego of his own on 160 acres of land at the edge of the harbor, northwest of the spot Horton later chose. Although folks in Old Town sarcastically referred to the project as "Davis's Folly," the development was at first a moderate success, attracting the interest of, among others, the U.S. Government, which built a military base and barracks in the new district. Unfortunately, the area lacked fresh water, which not surprisingly turned away many would-be settlers from the subdivision. By the time a well was dug in 1861, the Civil War had taken the soldiers away and the development was abandoned.

Unaware of what fate had in store for them, Davis and his partners purchased a number of prefab houses in San Francisco, which they planned to sell to the throngs of newcomers who were expected to settle in the San Diego area. The William Heath Davis House was the first such building erected in the new district and is today the only one still standing. Free tours of the Gaslamp Quarter depart from the house every Saturday morning. Call 233-5227 for current tour times. The other holdover from the days of Davis's Folly is Pantoja Park, at the corner of

Columbia and G Streets. According to Davis's scheme, Pantoja was supposed to be the hub of the new development, with streets radiating out in all directions. Today, it is the oldest park in San Diego outside of Old Town and a reminder of Davis's premature plans.

San Diego's oldest office building is located here in the Gaslamp Quarter, on the corner of Fifth Avenue and G Street. Built in 1874 to house the Consolidated National Bank, the two-story building became, over time, the main branch of the San Diego Public Library. The third and fourth stories were added in the early 1890s, when other municipal offices moved in and the building became San Diego's City Hall. The chambers of the mayor and councilmen remained here until 1938, when city offices were relocated to the spacious new Art Deco building on Harbor Drive.

A few steps north, on the right-hand side, is the twin-spired Louis-Bank of Commerce Building, erected in 1888, during the most feverish days of the boom. During San Diego's Stingaree days, the Louis-Bank of Commerce Building housed the Golden Poppy Hotel, a bizarre brothel where patrons chose from a selection of *filles de joie*, clad in outfits color-coordinated to match the bedrooms.

Just east of the Gaslamp is the San Diego Farmers' Bazaar, set in an old steel warehouse on the corner of Seventh Avenue and K Street in the heart of San Diego's wholesale produce district. Open every day except Monday, this fruit, flower, vegetable, seafood, and meat market is the genuine article, attracting restaurateurs and locals with its vast selection, high energy, and low prices. Many of the warehouses surrounding the market have been converted into artists' lofts, adding to the neighborhood's busy, Bohemian feel.

When you return to the Gaslamp, go east along G Street. This will bring you into the G Street arts corridor, a seven-block collection of galleries and shops featuring the work of local artists and artisans. Beyond the galleries, at 15th Avenue and E Street, is a huge building now owned by Jerome's Furniture. From the 1920s to the 1940s, this was the Coliseum Athletic Club, where professional boxing matches were held each Friday night before sellout crowds. If you look closely, you can just make out the old ticket windows, now bricked up, where anxious fans queued to see the likes of Archie Moore, the San Diego-born light-heavyweight legend who still holds the world record for knockouts at 129.

Golden Hill, Cortez Hill, and Banker's Hill

East of downtown along Broadway and side streets is Golden Hill, one of the city's oldest residential neighborhoods and a treasure trove of gingerbread Victoriana. It was here, during the late nineteenth century, that many San Diegans moved to escape the craziness of the city's core, constructing giant homes with panoramic views of downtown and the bay. When the neighborhood was originally settled, the sale of alcoholic beverages was prohibited, as were barns and farm animals. When fashions changed and the city's finest abandoned Golden Hill for Mission Hills and La Jolla in the late 1920s, the liquor stores moved in and the neighborhood began a slide that continued for almost fifty years. Recently, a whole new generation of locals has taken to Golden Hill, buying up the large properties here and renovating them. Although these efforts are beginning to pay off, Golden Hill still has a distinctly shabby side and some of the former mansions are little more than tenements, held together by old paint and the rapacity of absentee landlords. Still, the neighborhood is worth a visit, by car if possible so that you can take in Cortez and Banker's Hills as well. Generally speaking, most of the renovated homes are north of Broadway, but the larger and more interesting mansions are east of 21st Street, between C and F streets.

The Quartermass-Wilde house on the corner of Broadway and 24th Street is a Queen Anne Victorian residence built in 1896 by Ruben Quartermass, a successful local businessman. In 1907, the mansion was purchased by Louis J. Wilde, the mayor of San Diego and the man who financed the Horton Plaza fountain. When Wilde bought the house it was located on the corner of 24th and D streets. Wilde didn't like the sound of "D Street"—it had a dull and underachieving ring to it—so he changed the street's name to Broadway, which provided him with an address as lofty as his ambitions.

Farther south, at the corner of 20th and K streets, is Villa Montezuma, an example of ornate Victorian styling and overwrought civic boosterism. Designed by Comstock and Trotsche and financed by a group of affluent San Diegans, the Villa was presented to Jesse Shepard in 1887, to lure the internationally acclaimed writer and musician to San Diego. The scheme worked for a time, though Shepard's creative output during his San Diego years—which was confined to holding seances—must have disappointed his wealthy backers. A fire in the mid-1980s did minor damage to the structure but it has been repaired. Today, the house is operated by the San Diego Historical Society. If stained glass, brass fixtures, redwood walls, and flaky former residents appeal to you, you can take a guided tour ($3) of Villa Montezuma Wednesday through Sunday from 1 to 4. Women should note that high-heeled shoes cannot be worn inside. Call 239-2211 for more information.

Two neighborhoods north of downtown provide another glimpse into San Diego's past. Cortez Hill, the four-block area surrounding the El Cortez Hotel, is particularly rich in California bungalows and aging Spanish colonial revival apartment buildings. During the 1880s and '90s, prominent San Diegans built homes here to take advantage of the breathtaking views. Another spurt of growth occurred between 1913 and 1915, when a number of apartment complexes were built in anticipation of the Panama-California Exposition. In those days, Interstate 5 didn't cut Cortez Hill off from nearby Balboa Park, and visitors could walk two blocks and into the southern end of the fair.

The towering El Cortez Hotel, built in 1927, dominates the neighborhood. For many years the El Cortez was the premier hotel in the San Diego area and its fifteenth-floor Skyroom was *the* place to bring out-of-town guests for dinner or after-theater cocktails. Sadly, the hotel fell apart during the 1960s, passing through a number of hands and finally giving up the ghost. In 1978, the building was purchased by evangelist Morris Cerullo, who used it as world headquarters for his ministry. During the 1980s, the hotel was purchased by a local businessman who, together with a Japanese firm, planned to redevelop Cortez Hill as an upscale neighborhood with a revamped El Cortez as its centerpiece. The partnership split in 1990, however, when the Japanese partners insisted that the old hotel had to be razed; the local boy—who, fortunately, held title—refused to be an accomplice to that brand of mindless civic destruction. Today, the hotel lies abandoned and its future remains uncertain. The building has, however, been declared "historically significant," making imminent demolition unlikely.

Farther north of downtown, just west of Balboa Park on an "island" created by a series of converging canyons, is Banker's Hill, an area popular with San Diego's wealthier citizens over the years. At one time, this genteel area was known as "Pill Hill" because so many local doctors ran practices out of their homes here; today, the area just east of Banker's Hill still contains a number of medical offices and diagnostic labs.

Although Banker's Hill is just west of Balboa Park, it nevertheless is quite difficult to reach by car, thanks to the aforementioned canyons. But the neighborhood is worth touring, if only to see the many craftsman-style homes designed by noted San Diego architect Irving Gill. Your best bet is to take Fifth Avenue north from downtown to Brookes Avenue. Turn left on Brookes, turn left again on Front Street, and then take a right on Walnut. From there, the streets wind down through Banker's Hill, terminating at Reynard Way. When you get to Reynard, head south. Turn right on Laurel and take it up to Balboa Park. If you're on foot, Banker's Hill is easily accessed via the Spruce Street bridge, located right off Front Street at Spruce Street, one of the many footbridges built during the late nineteenth and early twentieth centuries to connect canyon-surrounded neighborhoods with the electric streetcars that crisscrossed San Diego. The bridge at Fourth Avenue and Quince Street is the only other surviving footbridge from the period.

Fans of the macabre might consider stopping by 406 Nutmeg Street, the two-story colonial brick house where in 1989 divorcée Betty Broderick murdered her ex-husband and his new wife in bed, a killing portrayed in the made-for-TV movie *A Woman Scorned*. Take First Avenue north to Palm Street. Turn left on Palm and follow the street until it ends. The scene of the crime is on your right. On your way back to Laurel Street, stop by the Long-Waterman house, an ornate Victorian mansion on the corner of First Avenue and Laurel which still serves as a private residence. The Sherman Gilbert house, another beautiful Banker's Hill mansion, has been moved from its original location at Second and Fir streets to Heritage

Park in Old Town, but Temple Beth Israel, one of the oldest synagogues in California, remains on the corner of Third Avenue and Laurel.

Balboa Park

Just northeast of downtown, in an area roughly bounded by Sixth Avenue to the west and Park Boulevard to the east, is Balboa Park, San Diego's premier recreational and cultural spot. Originally known as City Park, this 1,400-acre urban oasis was first set aside in 1868, when there were fewer than 2,500 people living in the city. Although it was threatened by speculators during the real-estate madness of the 1880s, the park remained untouched—and largely unimproved—until 1892, when Kate Sessions, a woman whose green thumb left its imprint in Coronado, Pacific Beach, Horton Plaza, and Mission Hills, was retained by the city to enhance a small portion of the western half of the park. The beautification projects continued over the years, transforming the 600-acre western section of the park into a stunning greenbelt of manicured lawns, shady eucalyptus groves, and towering palms.

Although the structures appear to date from a much earlier era, most of Balboa Park's buildings were in fact erected in 1915 for the Panama-California Exposition, which celebrated the opening of the Panama Canal and was the first architecturally unified exposition ever. Designed by Bertrand Goodhue on Spanish, Mexican, and Moorish models, the buildings transformed the empty park into a magnificent Spanish "city" and were admired by a number of important visitors to the fair, including William Jennings Bryan, Theodore Roosevelt, Thomas Edison, and Henry Ford. But no one was more enchanted with Goodhue's work than San Diegans themselves. Though these buildings were meant to be temporary ex-

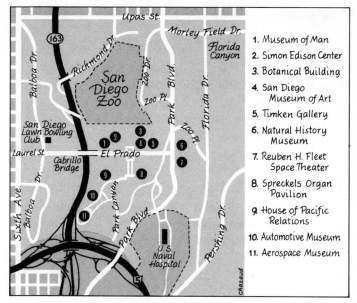

1. Museum of Man
2. Simon Edison Center
3. Botanical Building
4. San Diego Museum of Art
5. Timken Gallery
6. Natural History Museum
7. Reuben H. Fleet Space Theater
8. Spreckels Organ Pavilion
9. House of Pacific Relations
10. Automotive Museum
11. Aerospace Museum

Balboa Park

hibit halls only, locals grew so attached to the magnificent cream-colored *palacios* that they refused to tear them down. The structures came in handy again during the 1935 California-Pacific International Exposition and have served the city in a variety of capacities ever since. Today, they house Balboa Park's twelve museums, six theaters, and three galleries and form one of the largest arts complexes in the U.S. outside the Mall in Washington, D.C.

The park's main entrance is located off Sixth Avenue at Laurel Street. On the left are the playing fields of the San Diego Lawn Bowling Club, which stages matches on the two bowling greens here at 12:30 every day, except Sunday. To the right is an area known as the "Fruit Loop"—a spot besieged by drug dealers, male hustlers, and undercover cops. Avoid it unless you're in an automobile.

After crossing over the Cabrillo Bridge, with its 1,500-foot span and cantilevered archways, you pass through

El Portal, the grand entrance to Balboa Park and onto *El Prado* (Span., the Walk), the park's main east-west thoroughfare. The tablet above the archway, with its male and female figures and civic crest, celebrates the opening of the Panama Canal and San Diego's position as the first major port on the Pacific side.

To the left is the California Building, with its exquisitely domed, 200-foot bell tower and busts commemorating the explorers and missionaries who played a role in the city's settlement and development. Adjacent to the tower is the Museum of Man, originally established under the auspices of the Smithsonian. Its exhibits include masks, costumes, weapons, and artifacts from North, Central, and South America—many of them collected for the 1915 exposition—as well as plaster reproductions of Mayan sandstone monuments. During World War II, when much of Balboa Park was pressed into national service and dubbed "Camp Kidd," the Museum of Man was one of three museums in the park that served as hospitals, handling overflow patients from the nearby Naval Hospital. When hostilities ended in 1945, the exhibits were taken out of storage and returned. Admission to the Museum of Man is $3 for adults, $1 for teenagers, and 25 cents for kids. Consider purchasing a visitor's Passport, a $9 pass that permits entry into up to four of the Balboa Park museums. These passes are available from the Balboa Park Visitors Center at 1549 El Prado (239-0512).

Directly behind the Museum of Man is the Simon Edison Center for the Performing Arts, the home to San Diego's world-famous Old Globe Theater. Originally built to mount what were derisively called "tabloid" productions of Shakespeare during the 1935 exposition, the Old Globe gradually developed into a legitimate operation. Today, it is home to the only professional Shakespearean repertory company on the West Coast.

As it cuts through Balboa Park, El Prado is lined with galleries and museums. Some are definitely worth a visit. The San Diego Museum of Art (232-7931) and the Timken Gallery (239-5548), though not in the same league as New York's Metropolitan or LA's Getty Museum, are nevertheless interesting and fairly well-endowed. The Timken is the only museum in Balboa Park that doesn't charge for admission, and it has a fine collection of Russian icons, French Gobelin tapestries, and European and American masterpieces. The Natural History Museum, adjacent to the park's main fountain, is another safe bet, featuring dinosaur skeletons, a giant whale, and an array of hands-on displays kids love, including a live-reptile exhibit in the Desert Discovery Lab. Admission is $3 for adults, $1 for teenagers, and 25 cents for children. Call 239-2001 for more information.

The Reuben H. Fleet Space Theater and Science Center, across El Prado from the Natural History Museum, features an Omnimax dome screen projector and interactive science exhibits. Admission is $5.50 for adults and $3 for kids. Call 238-1168 for information.

The House of Hospitality, opposite the Timken Gallery, houses one of the park's few restaurants, the Cafe Del Rey Moro (Span., Cafe of the Moorish King), which overlooks a secluded patio where many local couples have exchanged wedding vows over the years. The inner courtyard, modeled after a convent patio in Guadalajara, Mexico, features a sculpture of an Aztec woman, fashioned from limestone by Donal Hord, the artist whose work is featured in front of the County Administration Building on Harbor Drive. Clean restrooms are located in the courtyard.

A few steps from the House of Hospitality, at the northern end of *La Laguna de las Flores* (Span., Lake of the Flowers), is the park's massive Botanical Building. This redwood lath house, supported by an iron skeleton designed for use in a Santa Fe Railroad station, features over five hundred tropical and subtropical plants and is a good place to cool off on sizzling summer afternoons.

South of the House of Hospitality, just past Anna Huntington's statue, *El Cid*, are the Spreckels Organ Pavilion, the House of Pacific Relations, and the Aerospace Museum. Built by John D. and Adolph B. Spreckels, the elaborately ornamented organ pavilion houses the largest outdoor pipe organ in the world. The free concerts on Sunday afternoons have been a San Diego tradition since the instrument was dedicated in 1914. The House of Pacific Relations, located just west of the pavilion, is actually 15 small cottages, originally used by the nations participating in the 1935 exposition. Today, the cottages have been turned over to expatriates from some twenty-four nations, who use the small huts as meeting halls and gathering places. On Sundays, the cottages are open to the public, and costumed immigrants demonstrate their native customs and traditions. Keep your eye out for the periodic festivals here. During these colorful and tasty weekend affairs, the local expatriates dress up in their traditional clothes, prepare and sell exotic foods, and perform the songs and dances of their native lands.

The Aerospace Museum, located just beyond the House of Pacific Relations, exhibits a collection of aircraft and memorabilia from the early days of flight and chronicles the important contributions San Diego has made to the development of aviation.

The San Diego Zoo, which began as a modest zoological exhibit at the 1915 exposition, is located at the northeastern end of Balboa Park, just past Spanish Village. Over four thousand animals—one of the largest and most comprehensive collections in the world—are on display inside the zoo's 125-acre compound. Most of the animals roam about in semifreedom, separated from human visitors by little more than moats. The Children's Zoo, the reptile house, the koala, tiger, sun bear, and gorilla exhibits, and the walk-through aviaries are outstanding and justly famous. The zoo is open daily from 9 to 5. Admission is $12 for adults and for $4 for the kids. Call 234-3153 for more information.

Most of the museums and institutions in Balboa Park (except the zoo) offer free admission at least one day a month. To simplify things, the museums have chosen Tuesday as bargain day. On the first Tuesday of each month, the San Diego Natural History Museum and the Science Center at the Reuben H. Fleet Space Theater offer free admission. On the second Tuesday of each month, the Museum of San Diego History, the San Diego Hall of Champions Sports Museum, and the Museum of Photographic Arts offer free admission. On the third Tuesday of each month, the Museum of Man and the San Diego Museum of Art are open for free. And on the fourth Tuesday of each month, the San Diego Aerospace Museum and the San Diego Automotive Museum offer free admission.

If you're interested in exerting yourself, don't overlook the other half of Balboa Park, on the eastern side of Florida Canyon. Though less developed, and less frequented by visitors, the eastern section offers a swimming pool, public golf course, hiking trails, a frisbee golf course, and—bicycle enthusiasts take note—one of the largest velodromes in North America. Because the area has not undergone extensive development, the shrub-covered canyons and mesas here provide a glimpse of the landscape the Kumeyaay roamed before Spanish contact.

At the northwestern end of Balboa Park, just north of Upas Street on Seventh Avenue, are a number of homes built by Irving Gill, the San Diego architect credited with creating a unique California style of simplified Spanish motifs and stucco. The Marston House at 3525 Seventh Avenue (298-3142), one of Gill's masterpieces, is operated by the San Diego Historical Society and open to the public.

Chapter Five
♦♦♦♦♦♦♦♦♦♦♦

Old Town Wanderings

FOR MOST of the fifty years of the Spanish period, San Diego remained an isolated religious and military outpost. Outside the presidio's community of soldiers and the mission's community of priests and neophytes, there was nothing but "wild" Indians and barren countryside for hundreds of miles.

Things changed toward the end of the Spanish period. Soldiers from the presidio began to move down into the river flats below the fort, where they cultivated small plots and erected makeshift huts. Captain Francisco Maria Ruíz is believed to have started the trend, building a small adobe house in the valley around 1820. Other soldiers soon followed, creating the scattered beginnings of what today is called Old Town. Most of the buildings erected during the Spanish period were modest affairs, with mud walls and dirt floors; certainly nothing as substantial as a two-story structure was raised during those years. The presidio, mission, and old mission dam were the only large-scale construction projects undertaken by the Spaniards. Today, only the mission and dam remain.

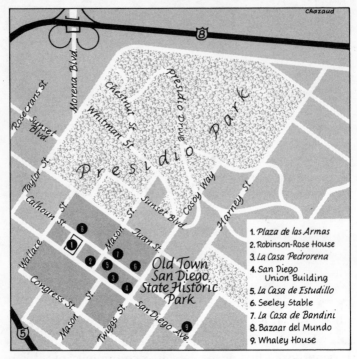

1. Plaza de las Armas
2. Robinson-Rose House
3. La Casa Pedrorena
4. San Diego
   Union Building
5. La Casa de Estudillo
6. Seeley Stable
7. La Casa de Bandini
8. Bazaar del Mundo
9. Whaley House

Old Town San Diego

Old Town began to flourish and expand during the Mexican period, when the three thousand square miles of mission lands in San Diego were secularized and turned into private *ranchos*. As the new owners prospered from the growing cattle trade, they built large, rambling adobe houses in the tiny pueblo. Inside these impressive homes the visitor would find, in the words of one historian, all the "dignity, elegance, refinement and charm of people reared in the capitals of the old world."

The number of families constituting this new upper class was quite small. For the most part San Diego remained a poor, dull village, in sharp contrast to its spectacular surroundings. With few exceptions, such as *La Casa de Estudillo* (Span., the Estudillo House) and *La*

Casa de Bandini (Span., the Bandini House), the adobe structures in the city were crude and unimpressive affairs. Surveying San Diego in the mid-1830s, Richard Henry Dana, Jr., author of *Two Years Before the Mast*, saw little to write about, just "forty dark brown looking huts . . . and three or four larger ones, white-washed."

The central *Plaza de las Armas* (Span., Plaza of Arms), bounded by Wallace Street, Calhoun Street, Mason Street, and San Diego Avenue, was set aside in the early 1820s, in an attempt to impose a sense of order and direction on the chaotic, sprawling pueblo. In later years, homes and stores were built around the plaza and it came to serve as the town's hub. Celebrations, bullfights, rodeos, military displays, and official and semiofficial ceremonies of all kinds were held here, and villagers often pulled themselves onto the roof of La Casa de Estudillo to get a better view of these events. The flagpole—fashioned from a ship's mast—that stands at the southern end of the plaza marks the spot where Marines from the USS *Cyane* raised the Stars and Stripes on July 26, 1846, ushering in the American period.

Old Town was forever changed by the arrival of the Americans. Although they were taken with the region's natural beauty, many of the Yankees who flooded into the area during the 1850s and '60s shared Mary Chase Walker's less-than-favorable impression of the town. Walker, who came to California from Massachusetts in 1854 to work as San Diego's first schoolteacher, described Old Town as "a most desolate looking" place. "[O]f all the dilapidated, miserable looking places," she wrote, "this is the worst."

As more and more Americans arrived in San Diego, they sought to remodel Old Town along more familiar and agreeable lines. The first to impose an American sense of order on the town's dusty Spanish landscape were members of the Mormon Battalion, sent west in 1846 to secure California in the war with Mexico. Although the soldiers made the 2,000-mile march from Council Bluffs, Iowa, to San Diego in record time, the struggle was concluded before they ever arrived. Undaunted, the battalion members went to work, whitewashing the adobe homes around the plaza (which they renamed "Washington Square") and generally doing their best to turn the pueblo into just another American town.

Later waves of immigrants continued the effort to make San Diego over in the image of a Boston or Peoria. They introduced "familiar" trees, like maple, hickory, and chestnut, and abandoned native building materials in favor of brick and wood. The low adobe huts, with their flat asphalted roofs, were quickly replaced by homes with high steep roofs and deep cellars. Street names were Americanized in short order as well. The desire to obliterate Spanish culture and recreate the architecture of the East was so great that some settlers purchased prefabricated homes in Maine—and waited while they were shipped around Cape Horn—rather than build from materials available locally. The Whaley House and the San Diego Union Building, both on San Diego Avenue, and the Robinson-Rose House, on Wallace Street, all date from this period.

Old Town fell on hard times during the 1870s and '80s, when Alonzo Horton's New Town and the arrival of the Santa Fe Railroad shifted attention away from the area. Some preservation was undertaken during the early twentieth century by the unflagging John Spreckels, and by a few others. But for the first two-thirds of the twentieth century Old Town was largely a run-down *barrio* (Span., neighborhood) of dilapidated homes and struggling businesses.

In 1968, the six-block core of Old Town was set aside as Old Town San Diego State Historic Park, and since then a number of buildings have been restored or reconstructed, including the Franklin House, the Colorado

House, and the San Diego Courthouse—the three buildings burned in 1872 by the fire that hastened the area's demise. As it stands today, Old Town is something of a historical amalgam, recreating San Diego as it might have appeared had the Mexican and the early-American periods occurred simultaneously.

Given Old Town's Spanish and Mexican past, it's not surprising that it's home to some of San Diego's best Mexican restaurants. These can be found on San Diego Avenue, on Congress Street, and within the confines of the park itself. Old Town is also a pleasant spot to browse and shop, particularly if you're in the market for the curious or exotic. The *Bazaar del Mundo* (Span., market of the world), a group of shops selling Southwestern and Mexican crafts, is at the northeastern end of the Plaza de las Armas, in a former auto court that has been delightfully renovated. (See "Shopping," pages 181–189.)

Until recently, the modern bothers of tight parking and traffic congestion dogged visitors to Old Town. Fortunately, the Metropolitan Transit Service plans to initiate trolley service to the area in the near future. Call the MTS (see "Transit System," pages 49–50) for more information. The blocks that make up the Old Town San Diego State Historic Park are closed to vehicular traffic, so come prepared to walk.

Robinson-Rose House

The two-story Robinson-Rose House, at the northern end of the Plaza de las Armas, was built in 1853 by James W. Robinson, a lawyer who came to San Diego from Ohio early in the American period and quickly became active in the town's political and legal affairs.

Robinson's background, which included a role in the Texas independence movement, gave him more than a passing understanding of the intricacies of both American and Mexican law. He rose to local prominence after Congress passed the Land Act of 1851, a law which compelled *rancheros* to secure legal confirmation of their land grants and provided unscrupulous Yankees with a potential tool for hoodwinking landowners out of their holdings. As litigation over land titles mushroomed in San Diego, Robinson's case load bulged and his reputation for integrity and expertise spread. Before he died in 1857, he had been involved in every aspect of civic life, serving as county attorney, school board member, and land commissioner, and helping found the Democratic Party in San Diego, which quickly became the party of choice in the small town. (This situation reversed itself after the arrival of Alonzo Horton. Horton, a Republican developer, announced that he would hire only Republicans on his construction projects. As one droll observer noted, "The Republican majority quite naturally grew by leaps and bounds.") Robinson was also closely associated with the doomed San Diego and Gila Railroad, an unsuccessful link between San Diego and the East; for a time, the Robinson-Rose building was known as the Railroad Building.

Although his San Diego neighbors never suspected it, Robinson had something of a checkered past. According to San Diego historian Ron Quinn, Robinson abandoned his first wife, Mary Isdell, and their three children, in Ohio in the late 1820s, in order to elope with Sarah Snyder, a woman he had met in a prayer meeting and would later bring with him to Texas and California. What's more, modern historians have had no luck figuring out where Robinson picked up his license to practice law, since there is no record of his having matriculated at any law school.

After Robinson died in 1857, his widow Sarah continued to live in the house, leasing out the extra rooms to a number of businesses, including the *San Diego Herald*. In

1868, Sarah sold the building to Louis Rose, an enterprising Texan who served for a time as postmaster in Old Town, and also ran a tannery and speculated in real estate. (The community of Roseville on Point Loma was one of Rose's real-estate developments.) Rose lived in the house until 1874, when a fire destroyed the roof. The house fell into ruin at the turn of the century and was not reconstructed until the mid-1980s. Today, the Robinson-Rose House serves as the headquarters for the park's rangers and features a large and quite useful diorama, which depicts Old Town's layout in its heyday during the mid-nineteenth century. A free, one-hour tour of the park—highly recommended—departs from the building each afternoon at 2.

La Casa de Estudillo

The best-preserved structure in Old Town is La Casa de Estudillo, a thick-walled adobe building across the Plaza de las Armas from the Robinson-Rose House. José Maria Estudillo, a retired commander of the presidio, began construction of the house in 1829. After he died the following year, his son, José Antonio Estudillo, continued adding new rooms around the inner courtyard, until 1850, when the house achieved the rambling shape it has today. The younger Estudillo lived here until 1887 with his wife and 12 children.

The timber for the beams supporting the tiled roof was carried down from the back country by Diegueño workers, who provided most of the labor for the project. Occasionally the Diegueños had to improvise. They molded the original roof tiles, for instance, by spreading wet clay on their legs. When the clay began to dry, it was removed and a new "tile" was ready. The Diegueños also avoided using nails—a scarce commodity in early San Diego—by binding together the beams of the house with leather fasteners. The exterior walls, made from adobe four-feet thick in some places, seemed crude, but they concealed and protected the opulence and luxury within.

Early this century, La Casa de Estudillo was rebuilt by John Spreckels, who also concocted the tale that the home was the marriage place of the heroine of Helen Hunt Jackson's 1884 novel, *Ramona*. Though unfounded, the legend proved to be an effective marketing scheme. For many years, dozens of "True Vow Keepers Clubs"— made up, according to Carey McWilliams, of couples who had been married fifty years or more—held their annual picnics at the house.

La Casa de Bandini

Just southeast of the plaza, along Calhoun Street, is La Casa de Bandini, an impressive two-story adobe home built in 1829 by Juan Bandini, the man whose political antics transformed San Diego into a den of intrigue against Mexican rule during the 1830s.

An Italian who came to California by way of Peru, Bandini was perhaps early San Diego's most colorful and amiable character. His wit and charm were legendary, and the village turned out regularly for the fiestas, celebrations, dances, and evening amusements he hosted at his residence. Games of chance were especially popular at these affairs, and, like his brother-in-law and neighbor, José Antonio Estudillo, Bandini often gambled to pass the time and stave off the boredom that hung like the morning fog over the isolated town. During the fight for California between the U.S. and Mexico, Bandini sided with the Americans, turning his house over to Commodore Stockton, who used it as his headquarters in 1846 and 1847. Legend has it Stockton was in La Casa de Bandini when Kit Carson raced into town with news of General Kearny's disastrous defeat at San Pasqual.

Originally, La Casa de Bandini was a one-story structure not unlike the neighboring La Casa de Estudillo. The second floor was built in 1869 by Albert Seeley, who had bought the home from Bandini after gambling debts forced Bandini to sell it. Seeley turned the building into the southern terminus for his successful San Diego–Los Angeles Stage Line. He added the second story and wraparound balcony to the structure, converting it to the Monterey style of architecture and giving it a new name: the Cosmopolitan Hotel.

Now part of the Old Town State Historic Park, La Casa de Bandini continues its commercial service, housing one of San Diego's best Mexican restaurants (see page 145). The inner courtyard, one of the most delightful dining spots in the city, is a lush, secluded garden patio with fine views of the building's architectural features. The exterior and much of the interior have been restored, evoking the building's mid-nineteenth–century grandeur.

Just west of La Casa de Bandini is the Seeley Stable, a reconstructed barn similar to the one used by Albert Seeley's stage line. The stable houses a collection of carriages, Western memorabilia, and Indian artifacts. A slide program about San Diego's early history is shown here three times daily.

San Diego Union Building

This wood-frame structure, located on San Diego Avenue near the western limits of Old Town State Historic Park, was one of the first of many prefabricated buildings shipped to San Diego from Maine in the early 1850s. The building served for many years as the residence of Miguel Pedrorena, who also erected the adjacent La Casa Pedrorena. In 1867, the structure was leased to the fledgling *San Diego Weekly Union*, which printed its first issue here on October 10, 1867. The paper continued to operate out of the house until 1870, when its offices were moved to Horton's Addition. The paper became a daily the following year.

The *Union* was San Diego's second newspaper; its first, the *San Diego Herald*, started publication in 1851, just 12 days after the *Los Angeles Star*, California's very first paper, rolled off the presses. In its early years, the *Herald* coasted along, doing about as well as an English-language paper could in a town with only seven hundred souls, half of whom could read only Spanish. But all that changed in 1853, when Lieutenant George Horatio Derby came to town. Sent to San Diego to build a dam that would divert floodwaters away from San Diego Bay and into *Bahia Falsa*, as Mission Bay was known in those days, Derby avoided the long hike to and from the site by renting a two-story house on the edge of Old Town and supervising construction from his second-story bedroom window. With the extra time, the young man dedicated himself to literary pursuits, penning short humorous stories for his own enjoyment. Within six months of his arrival, Derby had so impressed locals with his cleverness and uncommon sense that John Judson Ames, the *Herald*'s editor, entrusted the paper to the young man when business took him to San Francisco for six weeks. Writing under various names, including "John Phoenix" and "John Q. Squibob," Derby turned the *Herald* inside out, introducing humor and sarcasm to its pages and turning the paper's editorial philosophy on its head. For one issue, Derby produced the "Phoenix Illustrated Edition," a good-natured jab at the illustrated newspapers which were growing in popularity at the time. When Ames returned to San Diego, he kept Derby on. In 1855, Ames published *Phoenixiana*, a collection of Derby's best writing from the *Herald*, and the book sold well on both coasts. Later, a second volume, called *The Squibob Papers*, appeared.

Derby eventually purchased the *Herald*, running the operation out of the Rose-Robinson House. When he was transferred out of San Diego in 1855, Derby left the paper in the hands of editor William Noyes, who received two-thirds of the returns for his stewardship. With its resident wit gone, however, the paper languished and in 1860 the *Herald* ceased publication. Squibob Square, the collection of shops across San Diego Avenue from the San Diego Union Building, is named in honor of Derby.

Presidio Park

When the Spaniards arrived in San Diego in 1769, they established their first settlement on this hill, just east of what would become Old Town. With its sweeping views of the San Diego River valley and the coast, the spot afforded obvious advantages to the tiny Spanish garrison that was posted here to ensure that California remained out of British and Russian hands. Although Junípero Serra eventually was compelled to move *La Mision de San Diego de Alcalá* six miles up the valley, the military remained in *El Presidio Real* (Span., the Royal Garrison) for the duration of the Spanish occupation, though the fort steadily crumbled over time.

The deterioration continued during the Mexican period, but the presidio continued to be a useful stronghold until the mid-1830s. By then it was a shambles, the victim of looting by unpaid local officials and disregard by the authorities in Mexico. The Mexican government billeted the last group of soldiers to the dilapidated garrison in 1837; in that year, the last contingent, described by one observer as a squad of "half clothed and half starved-looking fellows," was reassigned to Los Angeles.

A second fort was built on this hillside in 1838, when Old Town residents became concerned about the possibility of Indian attacks on their pueblo. Inasmuch as the Mexicans were treating the Diegueños as chattel, these fears were not entirely baseless. The expected uprising didn't take place, however, until November of 1851, when Antonio Garra, a chief of the Cupeño Indians in North County, was incited to revolt by an unscrupulous trader. The Warner Ranch was attacked and several people were killed, but Garra and his confederates were quickly captured, tried, and executed. In 1846, when American forces landed in San Diego, the fort on the hillside was occupied by Commodore Samuel Francis du Pont. Later that year, Commodore Robert Stockton took charge of the stronghold, reinforcing its fortifications and renaming the fort after himself.

The 37-acre park that surrounds the ruins of the presidio and the remnants of Fort Stockton was given to the city in 1929 by George Marston, a local businessman and the father of the San Diego Historical Society (SDHS). Marston also built the Junípero Serra Museum, the Mission Revival–style building that dominates the park and is often mistaken for the mission, as a monument to the city's rich Hispanic heritage. For many years, the building served as the headquarters of the SDHS; today it operates as a museum dedicated to the history of San Diego. Its site is believed to be the place where Junípero Serra raised his cross. The museum is open Tuesday through Saturday from 10 to 4:30 and Sundays from noon to 4:30.

El Jupiter, the 2,000-pound cannon that proudly guarded Presidio Park for years, was recently removed from the park for a much-needed restoration. Cast in the Philippines in 1783 and brought to San Diego by the Spanish to protect the mouth of San Diego Bay, El Jupiter was moved to the Plaza de las Armas in the 1840s, where it fired ceremonial salutes. When the work on the cannon is completed, it will be displayed in the Junípero Serra Museum together with its massive wooden mount.

La Mision de San Diego de Alcalá

Six miles east of Presidio Park and Old Town is *La Mision de San Diego de Alcalá*. Today the site contains the restored chapel and outbuildings of San Diego's second mission. In 1774, Junípero Serra moved the mission from its temporary location inside the presidio to this site, near a Diequeño village called Nipaguay, in order to remove the Indians from the baneful influence of the soldiers and to place the mission closer to arable land.

The new setting was an improvement, but the relocated mission lasted less than a year. In 1775, about four hundred Diegueños attempted to drive the priests from the region, attacking the mission and setting fire to the new chapel. One of the Franciscans, Father Luis Jayme, made the mistake of walking into the ranks of the attackers with his arms outstretched, saying "Love God, my children." The Diegueños clubbed him to death. Serra reportedly reacted to Jayme's martyrdom by exclaiming, "Thanks be to God. That land is already irrigated; now the conversion of the Diegueños will succeed."

Serra was right. Within a year, the Franciscans had baptized four hundred Diegueños and begun construction of a new mission on this site. The new mission was completed in 1780. Vineyards, olive groves, and fruit trees were planted around the mission and neophytes were put to work herding cattle and sheep in the neighboring valleys. Unfortunately, Mision de San Diego de Alcalá continued to be dogged by bad luck. In 1803, an earthquake sent shock waves through the region, bringing the unreinforced mission down on the heads of the priests. But even this setback did not deter the Spaniards, who rebuilt the mission yet again, completing the job ten years later. In this incarnation, the mission flourished, expanding its land and animal holdings and increasing Indian conversions. By 1831, the handful of priests and their 1,700 Indian charges controlled 8,000 head of cattle, 1,200 head of horses and mules, 17,000 sheep, and more than 3,000 square miles of land.

But with the Mexican policy of secularization, the mission declined swiftly. Visiting San Diego in 1835, just one year after the policy came into effect, Richard Dana saw only emptiness and ruin. The decay continued during the American period. Used for a short time by U.S. Army troops as a barracks, the mission eventually was abandoned. Settlers picked over the ruins for timber and bricks and by the beginning of this century the mission was in decidedly sad shape.

In 1931, the mission was reconstructed along the lines of the 1803 mission. It has a three-story campanile with five belfries, and "cracks" and exposed bricks to create the illusion of age. La Mision de San Diego de Alcalá is open daily from 9 to 5, but because it still is a parish church, the chapel is closed to sightseers during Mass on Sundays. The easiest way to reach the mission is by taking Interstate 8 east to Fairmont Drive. Go north on Fairmont Drive and then west on Twain Avenue.

Chapter Six
♦♦♦♦♦♦♦♦♦♦

Beaches and Coastal Communities

S AN DIEGO has some of the nicest oceanfront property on earth. Yet, the Spaniards who settled here in
the late 1760s don't seem to have been impressed by this
fact. They built their first mission five miles away from
the nearest beach; then, in 1775, they moved even farther
inland, a full ten miles east of the breaking surf.

This bizarre settlement pattern continued well into the
1880s, during both the Mexican and American periods.
When Alonzo Horton finally willed downtown San Diego
to its present location, in 1867, he placed his New Town
closer to the vital harbor but even farther away from the
area's beaches.

The Kumeyaay weren't as oblivious to San Diego's
stunning coastline. They recognized a good thing when
they saw it, and, like the La Jolla and San Dieguito Indians
before them, the Kumeyaay spent much of their time on
area beaches. For half the year—usually during the winter—they camped near the shore, frolicking in the surf,
basking in the sun, and feasting on shellfish and scallops
caught offshore.

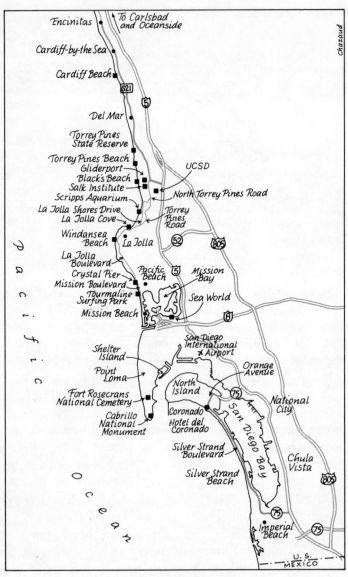

Coastline and Beaches

The settlement of San Diego's coastal corridor began tentatively in the late 1880s, in Coronado, Pacific Beach, and La Jolla. It didn't pick up sustained momentum until the 1950s and '60s, when thousands of defense-industry employees flooded into the new communities that were being dredged out of Mission Bay.

Today, the beach area is the city's principal recreational destination, for natives and newcomers alike. In the summer, the 55-mile-long coastline that stretches from Oceanside to the Mexican border is awash in swimmers, sunbathers, surfers, and strollers. During the winter months, violent Pacific storms generate waves, which tear away at the beach, exposing the underlying rocks and discouraging all but the most inveterate beachgoers from venturing down to the coast. But even in winter, San Diego's beaches offer plenty of opportunities for fun. There is, for instance, no better place on earth to catch the annual migration of gray whales than from oceanside bluffs in the city. During the day, there are tidepools, teeming with life, to explore. And when the sun sets, there are spawning grunion to catch.

Starting just north of La Jolla, you can hike through the gnarled splendor of Torrey Pines State Reserve. Heading south, you can catch the swimsuit-optional action at notorious Black's Beach, or visit Scripps Aquarium and the neighboring village of La Jolla. South of La Jolla, you can tackle Mission Bay's 4,600 acres of beaches and parkland, retrace Cabrillo's steps on Point Loma, and then continue down to Mexico through the exclusive "island" of Coronado. Along the way, you can stop your car and wade into the surf at any one of the dozen or so state and local beaches on the route. At some locations, coastal access may seem to be blocked by residential developments, but clearly marked public pathways leading down to the sand are seldom very far away.

Here are some reminders to help you enjoy the area's

beaches. Remember that it's always best to consult the lifeguard before wading into unknown waters (and, see "Rip Tides," page 47). At many beaches, separate areas are set aside for swimmers and surfers; you can avoid a lot of trouble by talking with the lifeguard first. Also, don't forget to pick up after yourself. Trash left on the beach provides ammunition to the small but vocal "locals-only" crowd that blames outsiders for all the coast's ills. They're wrong, of course, but this is one of those instances where perception counts as much as reality. Help change the perception by disposing of your trash properly, even if it means hauling it back to your house or hotel room.

If you decide to explore the tidepools, wear shoes with a thick, nonskid sole, tread carefully, and prepare to get wet. Tidepooling is definitely a hands-on activity, and you should feel free to turn over rocks and pick up sea life. But remember to put things back where you found them so that others can enjoy. The California Fish and Game Code forbids the removal of objects from area tidepools.

Torrey Pines State Reserve

This 2,500-acre reserve, perched on the cliffs overlooking the ocean just north of La Jolla, is one of only two places on earth where the twisted, majestic Torrey pine grows. The other spot is Santa Rosa, an uninhabited island belonging to the Channel Islands chain, about thirty miles off the coast from Santa Barbara. Although La Jolla doesn't receive enough rainfall to support the thirsty Torrey pine, the trees have adapted well to the foggy coast. The Torrey's needles are shaped in such a way that they condense the fog droplets, providing just enough moisture to permit the tree to survive.

Dr. C. C. Parry, the official botanist for the International Boundary Survey, first identified the tree in the early 1850s, when he was in the region with a team of surveyors

platting the U.S.-Mexican border. But Parry, who named
the plant for his friend and fellow botanist John Torrey,
was by no means the first to discover the trees. During
the Spanish period, when low-lying scrub covered most
of San Diego, the Torrey pines on these rock-covered
bluffs served as landmarks for passing sailors, who called
the area *Punta de los Arboles* (Span., Tree Point). In
1889, the city of San Diego set aside over three hundred
acres here as a public park and established strict regulations to stop weekend picnickers from using the trees
for firewood—a not uncommon practice in those days.
During the next few decades the acreage of the reserve
increased, thanks in large part to Helen Browning Scripps,
the newspaper-heiress who purchased neighboring lands
and presented them to the city. Since the 1950s, the state
of California has operated the park. The admission charge
is $4.

The park's three thousand Torrey pines are best appreciated on the numerous trails in the main reserve. Favorites are the High Point Trail, a short walk that takes
you to the park's highest elevation, and Guy Fleming
Trail, a longer walk named for an early park keeper,
which features spectacular ocean views and scores of
Torrey pines, grotesquely twisted by the ocean winds. In
addition to being a good place from which to view the
December-to-February migration of California gray whales,
the park is also one of the best spots to catch a glimpse
of the dolphins that play and feed in the waters off San
Diego. Call 755-2063 for more information about guided
tours and picnicking policies at the reserve.

If you're a fan of the links, one look at the neighboring
Torrey Pines Municipal Golf Course will make you wish
you had brought your clubs along with you. If you decide
to play a few rounds at Torrey Pines you'll discover what
insiders already know: The two regulation-size par-72
courses here—arguably the best of the eighty or so courses

in the county—can play havoc with your handicap. The breathtaking scenery is so distracting that even the pros who play here each spring in the Shearson Lehman Hutton Open find themselves missing two-foot putts. Call 453-0380 for information on fees and tee times.

Black's Beach

Torrey Pines Beach, below the main reserve, is reached via the steep, mile-long Beach Trail. Once you finish the descent, you can either relax on the sand or head south, toward Black's Beach, San Diego's world-famous swimsuit-optional sunbathing spot.

Technically, nudity is not permitted at Black's, but you'd never know it by the number of unclad bodies bouncing around. Nude sunbathers first began coming to this isolated stretch of beach during the 1960s, when some folks took the mantra "Let It All Hang Out" very seriously indeed. By the early 1970s, so many people were playing nude volleyball, nude frisbee, and nude whatnot here that a reluctant city council legalized the practice, making Black's the only officially sanctioned nude beach in the nation.

In 1977, San Diego voters passed a ballot measure revoking Black's swimsuit-optional status. Police made a show of ticketing the undressed for a short time after the referendum, but there's barely any enforcement today.

The proximity of Black's Beach to UCSD is not entirely coincidental. Herbert Marcuse, the German philosopher, New Left leader, and author of *One Dimensional Man* and *Negations*, was a member of the university's faculty between 1965 and 1970. Among other things, Marcuse taught that nudity (and promiscuity) were important Marxist tactics that stripped away and exposed the repressive underpinnings of bourgeois society. As a result,

Black's Beach became a kind of Finland Station for over-zealous graduate students.

If you find widespread nudity more revolting than revolutionary, you'll prefer the beach at nearby La Jolla Shores, which is every bit as fine a stretch of sand as Black's Beach, though less secluded and considerably more crowded. During the nineteenth century, La Jolla Shores was used by smugglers bringing opium and Chinese laborers into California. Today the beach is popular with families and scuba divers, who suit up here before swimming out to the underwater reserve just offshore.

The Kumeyaay used to say the fish danced at La Jolla Shores on moonlit nights. As unlikely as it sounds, the event the Indians referred to was in fact real. It's part of the annual mating ritual of the grunion, a small, silvery fish found in local waters. On spring and summer evenings, shortly after midnight, the unusually high lunar tides wash thousands of grunion up on beaches up and down the coast here. Once ashore, the female grunion burrows her tail in the sand, well above the usual high-tide mark, laying eggs that are then fertilized by a gyrating male. When the spawning dance is finished, the adult fish return to the ocean. The incubation period of the eggs is timed to match the tides. By the time the moon brings the water back up to the eggs, they're ready to hatch and swim out to sea.

Catching these silvery fish as they spawn on the beach has been a local sport for decades. La Jolla Shores is one of the best spots to try your hand at it. But be sure to use your hands. Any other method, such as nets, buckets, or bags, is illegal. You're also supposed to have a California fishing license, though few people bother. If you decide to try to catch these slippery little fish, be prepared for disappointment: Though driven by nature to engage in this mating dance, the grunion don't oblige their human hunters by showing up at any one beach with regularity.

The skies above Black's Beach are often filled with gliders and hang gliders, held aloft by the strong onshore breezes. The craft take off from the Torrey Gliderport, located off Torrey Pines Road on Torrey Pines Scenic Drive, across the street from UCSD. The gliderport, perched 350 feet above the waves, has spectacular views of the coastline from Carlsbad to La Jolla. Glider enthusiasts insist the view is even better once you leave terra firma.

Next to the gliderport is the Salk Institute for Biological Studies, the laboratory home of Dr. Jonas Salk, the virologist who produced the first successful polio vaccine. Salk's efforts made him a hero and household name. But most Americans were in fact inoculated with a milder vaccine, developed by Albert Sabin, because Salk's formula—which used a live poliomyelitis virus—posed a threat to those who, for religious or other reasons, remained unvaccinated. Recently, Salk's formula has come back into favor, particularly in tropical countries. Today, the Salk Institute's two hundred researchers are working full-time on a number of new challenges, including the search for an AIDS vaccine.

Designed by the noted architect Louis Kahn, the Salk Institute's concrete and brick building is a striking expression of Kahn's concept of primitive monumentality. Along with the Richards Medical Research Building at the University of Pennsylvania, the Salk Institute is one of Kahn's best-known works in the West. Free 45-minute tours of the facility are conducted Monday through Friday, at 11 A.M., noon, 1 P.M., and 2 P.M. But this is, after all, a working lab, so tours are sometimes canceled for the good of science. Call 453-4100 *before* you make your plans.

Scripps Aquarium

Just south of Black's Beach on La Jolla Shores Drive are the Scripps Institution of Oceanography and the Scripps Aquarium. Both offer visitors a glimpse into state-of-the-art oceanographic research and a close look at some of the fascinating marine life that inhabits the waters off the California and Mexican coasts. Like so many of the cultural and scientific sites around La Jolla that bear the Scripps name—and some, like the Bishop's School, the La Jolla Library, and the La Jolla Women's Club, which do not—the institute and the aquarium were donated to the community by Helen Scripps. For her role in the growth and development of the area, Scripps was dubbed the "Fairy Godmother of La Jolla." Now operated by the Regents of the University of California, the aquarium is open from 9 to 5 daily. (The best time to visit is around 1:30, when the keepers feed the fish.) Outside the aquarium's front door is an artificial tidepool, complete with anemones and simulated tides, that provides a good introduction to the marine wonders found on area reefs. Admission is free, but donations of $3 for adults, $2 for seniors and teenagers, and $1 for children are encouraged. The pier just west of the aquarium is a favorite surfing spot for locals.

In early 1993, the present aquarium, which dates from 1950, will move into a spacious new home just up the hill and become the Stephen Birch Aquarium-Museum. The new complex will be about three times the size of the present aquarium and will feature an expanded tidepool exhibit, a 6,000-square-foot museum and an 11,000-square-foot aquarium. Call 534-3474 for more information.

La Jolla

Located on the northwest side of Mount Soledad, La Jolla is an exclusive seaside neighborhood of million-dollar homes and expensive boutiques. The origin of the neighborhood's name is a matter of some dispute, and there seems to be little hope of lifting the debate out of the realm of civic myth and legend. Locals, perhaps with their property values in mind, insist that the name derives from *La Joya* (Span., jewel). Others argue that it comes from the Kumeyaay word meaning "hidden cave" or "hollow." The latter explanation is supported by the presence of seven caves, just northeast of Prospect Street in La Jolla's Cove. These caves were accessible only by boat until 1904, when Gustav Schultz, a German geologist, carved out a land entrance to the largest cave. His 133-step passageway remains open today, though you'll have to pay the operators of a curio shop at the top to go down it. The cave is also known as "Sunny Jim Cave," a name given to it by early American visitors who thought its sea-level entrance looked like Sunny Jim, a well-known turn-of-the-century cartoon character. During Prohibition, the cave reportedly was used by bootleggers to cache contraband liquor smuggled north from Mexico aboard high-speed boats known as "rumrunners."

Archaeological finds suggest La Jolla was one of the places the Kumeyaay spent their winters, following in the footsteps of the La Jolla Indians who settled in the area five thousand or more years ago.

During the 1930s and '40s, hotels in La Jolla, like La Valencia on Prospect Street, catered to the rising stars of Hollywood. More stars followed in the '50s and '60s, when the La Jolla Playhouse, the local stage company founded by Gregory Peck and Mel Ferrer, brought actors to town for legitimate theater and a little fun.

Raymond Chandler lived and worked in La Jolla during

the 1940s and '50s. Some say that *Playback,* a novel Chandler finished shortly before his death in 1959, is set in La Jolla. Even today, you can meet in La Jolla the sort of characters you'd expect to find in a Chandler story: foreign remittance men, wayward heirs and heiresses, and anxious *nouveaux riches.*

One of the major attractions in La Jolla for locals and visitors is Prospect Street, a four-block row of upscale shops, restaurants, and galleries that offers plenty of opportunities for window-shopping and people-watching. Nicest of all, it is a pedestrian-oriented shopping district, a rarity in California. Because it's one of the hottest retail quarters in the city, competition on the street is fierce and the turnover is dizzying, making every trip a new experience. (See Chapters 9 and 11 for more information about eating and shopping in La Jolla.)

The other draw in La Jolla is the Cove itself, a rocky inlet popular with local swimmers and divers. In August each year, thousands of San Diegans take part in the La Jolla Rough Water Swim, an 80-year-old endurance contest that requires participants to swim from the Cove to Scripps Pier, out to sea, and then back to the Cove. The unclouded waters and amazing sea life here have attracted local swimmers for more than a century. During the waning days of the nineteenth century, the train that ran between San Diego and La Jolla was known as the "Abalone Express" because so many local divers used it to get to the Cove, where they dove for the once-plentiful abalone. These days, the clear waters of the Cove are part of protected underwater park. You're welcome to swim, snorkel, or scuba dive here, provided you don't take anything from the water. If you have kids in tow, there's a delightful children's pool on the edge of the Cove, yet another legacy of the generous Ms. Scripps.

To the south of the Cove, at 700 Prospect Street, is the San Diego Museum of Contemporary Art, which has a solid permanent collection but is at its best when hosting traveling exhibitions. Recent showings have included the works of Hans Haacke and a wide-ranging look at social-ist agit-prop posters, brought to town as part of San Diego's Soviet Arts Festival. The annual Festival of Ani-mation is screened in the museum's spacious theater, which is also home to a weekly Wednesday-night film series. Call 454-3541 for more information.

From Prospect, go south on La Jolla Boulevard, turning right on Nautilus Street and right onto Neptune Place. Stretched out before you is Windansea Beach, the spot where the loosely knit gang of surfers and drifters known as the "Mac Meda Destruction Company" held the wild beer bashes or "conventions" chronicled by Tom Wolfe in *The Pump House Gang*. Wolfe reportedly penned his in-depth exploration of California's hedonistic youth-and-surf culture without ever getting out of his trademark flashy duds. The beach continues to be a favorite spot for surfers and bodysurfers. To the north of Windansea Beach, stretching almost all the way back to La Jolla Cove, there are a number of tidepools filled with hermit crabs, mussels, sea urchins, and even the odd abalone and octopus. The best time to explore the tidepools is at low tide, when the reefs along the shore are exposed. When you go, you may see locals casting nets from exposed shoals offshore, trying to net the lobster and rock cod found in abundance here.

Mission Bay and Environs

Continuing south on La Jolla Boulevard, you'll wind past Tourmaline Surfing Park, a very popular surfing and windsurfing spot, and onto Mission Boulevard, the main north-south artery through Pacific Beach and Mission Beach and a good place to start your exploration of the western half of Mission Bay.

At the corner of Mission Boulevard and Garnet Avenue is Crystal Pier, a 700-foot promenade built in 1927. At the time, Pacific Beach was still a rural outpost of San Diego, famous for its orange and lemon groves and few nighttime amusements. None was more famous—or more short-lived—than the Crystal Ballroom, at the tip of Crystal Pier. With its cork floor, colorful wall murals, stunning setting, and swinging bands, the Crystal Ballroom became the destination of choice for local jazz-age flappers. Unfortunately, the dance hall and the pier were condemned only three months after they opened, when inspectors discovered that the pilings underneath already had been undermined by marine borers. Disappointed dancers foxtrotted their way over to the Mission Beach Ballroom, in John D. Spreckels's $4 million Mission Beach Amusement Center, but the magic of the Crystal Ballroom was never matched. Rebuilt in 1936, and again after devastating storms in 1982, Crystal Pier today boasts the only motel in the state where guests sleep over ocean waters. The beach to the south of the pier is very popular with local surfers and swimmers.

South on Mission Boulevard, past Pacific Beach Drive, is Mission Beach. Because parking here can be extremely tight, consider leaving your vehicle on one of the side streets in Pacific Beach and exploring Mission Beach on foot. The best way to accomplish this is by strolling up the boardwalk, the busy cement pathway that parallels the coast from the northern limits of Pacific Beach all the way down to the jetty in South Mission Beach. If you walk far enough south on the boardwalk, you'll pass by the remains of Spreckels's amusement park, now incorporated into a seaside shopping center known as Belmont Park. The recently renovated Giant Dipper roller coaster—the only ride of its kind to have careened onto the National Register of Historic Places—is again open for business, much to the pleasure of those who fondly remember when it served as the anchor for a full-blown fun zone here. The Plunge, Spreckels's giant indoor swimming pool, has been reopened as well. Admission to the pool is $1.25. Aside from these two reminders of its amusement park days, the boardwalk is free of the cheap amusements that have lingered on at similar promenades around the country.

If the hordes of skateboarders, skaters, joggers, bicyclists, and strollers on the boardwalk unnerve you, duck down any one of the delightful courts of Mission Beach. Many of these attractive residential side streets are closed to vehicular traffic, which makes exploring them on foot all the more enjoyable. If, on the other hand, you want to join the wheeled crowd, stop by Hamel's Action Sports Center at 704 Ventura Place, right behind Belmont Park's roller coaster. Hamel's is a family-oriented shop that has been renting skates and bikes to beachgoers for years. Well, it's a family-oriented business *most* of the time. The annual Miss Mission Beach Contest, arguably the raunchiest and rowdiest beauty contest on the planet, is sponsored each summer by Hamel's and held behind their store.

Mission Beach's charming courts give the neighborhood a village flavor, making it one of the most distinctive and popular spots in San Diego and concealing the fact that this is one of the city's most densely populated neighborhoods. Here, aging bungalows occupied by surfers abut million-dollar homes belonging to some of the city's most prominent citizens. What their occupants share is a love of the ocean and an ability to tolerate the weekend crowds, which can be maddening.

The courts continue on the eastern, or bay, side of Mission Boulevard, ending at a smaller and less crowded boardwalk on the edge of Mission Bay, San Diego's 4,600-acre public aquatic park. Even on the summer's busiest weekend, when the seaside boardwalk is snarled in pedestrian gridlock, the bayside remains relaxed and unruffled. It's a pleasant hangout for beachgoers looking to avoid the crowded oceanfront scene and an outstanding choice for families with young children.

Originally, Mission Bay was a vast lagoon into which the floodwaters of the San Diego River raced each winter. Not surprisingly, this made the bay's waters treacherous and unnavigable, and during the Spanish period the area was known as *Bahia Falsa*, or False Bay. Dikes built by the Americans during the late nineteenth century to divert the river's flood waters away from San Diego Bay made Bahia Falsa's situation even worse, sending silt and sediment into the bay and creating sandbars and mud flats that choked off its outlet to the ocean. Locals began to refer derisively to the area as "The Swamp." Some even began to use the bay as a dumping ground, gradually turning it into an eight-square-mile stagnant cesspool.

During the boom years of the 1880s, attempts were made to save the bay by developing the surrounding area. These efforts were largely unsuccessful. A contest held in 1888 to rename Bahia Falsa drummed up some interest in the area—and gave the bay the name it bears today—but the subsequent real-estate bust ended the ambitious plans for the area. Although resorts, amusement parks, and piers drew weekend visitors throughout the 1920s and '30s, the communities around the bay languished. As late as 1940, Mission Beach and Pacific Beach had only 2,500 residents between them.

Mission Bay was reborn during the late 1940s and early 1950s, when a flood-control channel diverted waters away from the area and a $2 million bond issue financed a thorough dredging of the bay. Today, the park's waters are a paradise for swimmers, boaters, water-skiers, jet-skiers, windsurfers and anglers. Its miles of landscaped shoreline are ideal for picnickers and strollers.

Sea World, the well-known home of the killer whales

Shamu and Baby Shamu, and of many penguins, sharks, dolphins, sea lions, moray eels, and other aquatic creatures, is located on the southern end of Mission Bay, at 1720 South Shores Road. The park, now operated by Anheuser Busch, is open daily from 9 A.M. to 11 P.M. during the summer and from 9 A.M. to dusk the rest of the year. Admission to San Diego's number one tourist attraction is $22 for adults, $17 for seniors, and $16 for children 3 to 16. (The admission fee does not include the cost of rides.) For more information call 226-3901.

Many sportfishing and whale-watching excursions leave from Quivera Basin, located west of Sea World off West Mission Bay Drive. Sportfishing boats provide all the gear you'll need, and the ships' crews will skin, smoke, freeze, and package whatever you're able to reel in. Rates for whale-watching and sportfishing excursions depend on the length of the trip. Companies offering parasailing adventures also operate from the Quivera Basin dock. Call 223-4386 for more information.

The Mission Bay Aquatic Center (488-1036) on Santa Clara Point in Mission Beach rents Hobie Cats, windsurfers, and sailboats at reasonable prices. The center has instructors on hand who can teach you everything you need to know about sailing, windsurfing, and water-skiing.

If you'd like to circle Mission Bay before you decide where to get out and stroll, follow Mission Boulevard south to West Mission Bay Drive. Turn left on West Mission Bay and get off at the Ingraham exit. Proceed north on Ingraham over one bridge. As you approach the second bridge, get in the left lane. Turn left onto Riviera Drive, left again on Pacific Beach Drive, and left onto Mission Boulevard. This round-the-bay tour should take about twenty minutes, though summer congestion can double your trip time.

Point Loma

Point Loma, the historic peninsula which encloses San Diego Harbor and protects it from ocean storms, is located west of downtown and south of Mission Bay. It was here, in 1542, that Juan Rodríguez Cabrillo came ashore and claimed the area, which he called *San Miguel*, for the King of Spain.

Since 1852, when Congress first set aside Point Loma as a military reservation, much of the seven-mile-long peninsula has been under the custodianship of the U.S. Army and Navy. During the late nineteenth and early twentieth centuries, extensive coastal fortifications were built on the steep slopes to guard San Diego Bay from enemy attack. By the mid-1930s, commanders considered the area impregnable. Today, most of the bunkers and gun emplacements have been dismantled or abandoned. With the exception of Fort Rosecrans National Cemetery, the area has reverted to its natural, chaparral-covered state.

Point Loma's major attraction today is Cabrillo National Monument, which commemorates the explorer's history-making visit here in 1542. The park commands magnificent views of downtown, North Island, Coronado, the Silver Strand, Tijuana, and Las Islas de los Coronados, a four-island wildlife sanctuary 15 miles south of San Diego in Mexican waters. Cabrillo National Monument is also one of the best places to watch the annual migration of California gray whales, which pass by here on their way from the Bering Sea to the warm lagoons of Baja. The visitor center is open from 9 A.M. to sunset during the summer and from 9 to 5 the rest of the year. It presents films and exhibits about the Spanish voyages of exploration, and offers information on the park's other points of interest. Brochures available at the center describe the flowers and other plants on the Bayside Trail, which winds along the eastern slope of the peninsula. The eastern side also has a number of tidepools to explore. Admission to the park is $3 per car or $1 per person if you arrive by bike or on foot. For more information call 557-5450.

Point Loma Lighthouse, also on the park's grounds, was originally constructed by the Americans from the adobe remains of Spanish coastal fortifications at *La Punta de los Guijarros* (Span., Cobblestone Point). For many years the lighthouse was known as the Old Spanish Lighthouse, in part because early light keepers took Mexican wives who spoke no English. During the 1860s, Old Spanish Lighthouse was a favorite weekend picnicking spot for San Diegans, who came in throngs to watch and cheer as locally based ships harpooned whales just off the coast here.

In fact, there are two lighthouses at Point Loma—one, built in 1891, still operates (but is closed to the public), while the other, built in 1854, is a museum. The 1854 structure stands as an amusing reminder that instant obsolescence is by no means a modern innovation. When it became operational in 1855, its keepers discovered that its beacon, perched about 450 feet *above* sea level, was useless, obscured by the clouds and fog that plague Point Loma during most of the year. This caused some embarrassment, of course, but it didn't ruffle the bureaucrats in charge, who were able to keep the fiasco under wraps for almost forty years. In 1891 a replacement was quietly built, closer to the water's edge.

Fort Rosecrans National Cemetery, located north of the park on both sides of Cabrillo Memorial Drive, is one of the largest military burial grounds in the nation. Over fifty thousand people are buried here, including some of the American soldiers and scouts who died at the disastrous showdown between Kearny and Pico in 1846 at the

Battle of San Pasqual. The remains of these casualties were originally interred at the battlefield, but in 1874 they were removed to the eastern side of Fort Rosecrans. The boulder that marks the gravesite of these soldiers was taken from the San Pasqual battlefield and placed here in 1922. The granite obelisk just north of the San Pasqual marker was erected in memory of the 60 sailors killed when the USS *Bennington* exploded in San Diego Harbor in July 1905. During the chilliest days of the Cold War, suspicious characters with Eastern European accents reportedly spent a lot of time visiting graves on the eastern slopes of the cemetery—and snapping photos of the Ballast Point nuclear submarine base below.

As you leave Cabrillo National Monument, turn right on Talbot Street and right again on Rosecrans Street. To the north is Roseville, a small, bayside neighborhood that until quite recently was home to the tight-knit community of Portuguese fishermen who operated San Diego's giant tuna fleet. To the south is *La Playa*, "the beach," a distinctive part of San Diego ever since the Mexican period. During the mid-nineteenth century, when the hide, tallow, and whale-blubber trades that were centered here prospered, they filled the air with the stench of rotting whale and cow carcasses. Today, both neighborhoods are on the exclusive side, with sweeping views of the bay and downtown skyline.

Coronado and the Silver Strand

Farther south, on the western side of the San Diego–Coronado Bay Bridge, is Coronado, a quiet, exclusive resort town with a decidedly insular feel. Originally, this palm-, cypress-, and pine-lined community was part of the city of San Diego, but in 1890 its residents, fed up with paying for services they didn't receive, voted to go it alone. For many years afterward, most visitors reached Coronado from San Diego by one of five ferries that plied the waters between the two cities, but when the toll bridge opened in 1969, the ferries were put out of business. Recently, the vessels have made something of a comeback, providing hourly service between the mainland and the Coronado peninsula. The ships leave San Diego on the hour and Coronado on the half-hour. Call 234-4111 for more information.

The main thoroughfare in Coronado is Orange Avenue, which runs past the community bandstand and through well-kept downtown Coronado, and then veers south, becoming state Route 74. The manicured lawns and well-ordered layout of the city are testaments to the important role high-ranking naval officers have played in Coronado's development.

The town's most famous landmark, the Hotel del Coronado, is at 1500 Orange Avenue. This rambling resort, with its cupolas, turrets, and charming inner courtyard, was built in 1888 and wired, legend has it, by Thomas Edison himself. Described as "airy, picturesque and half-bizarre" by Edmund Wilson, it quickly became an international destination of the first order, drawing diplomats, dignitaries, and royalty. Part of the Hotel del Coronado's attraction was its utter familiarity. The hotel's ornamental garden, its front-lawn rabbit hunts, and its staff (three hundred of whom were brought in from the east coast for the grand opening) were all intended to remind visitors from the east of the genteel resorts back home. But the Del was also romantic. It was here, in 1920, that the Prince of Wales—later King Edward VIII—met Wallis Simpson, then the wife of an American naval officer stationed in San Diego. The encounter began a lifelong romance that eventually cost King Edward his crown. The Hotel del Coronado, or the "Del" as it's known, has tried to make amends over the years by dedicating a number of rooms in the hotel to the Prince's memory. More recently, the Del has hosted a number of state affairs, including a 1972 dinner for President Richard Nixon and Mexico's President Gustavo Diaz Ordaz, reportedly the largest state dinner ever held outside the White House.

Since the earliest days of the motion-picture industry, Hollywood location scouts have "discovered" the Del over and over again, using it as an elegant backdrop for dozens of movies and television shows. *Some Like It Hot*, the 1958 comedy classic starring Jack Lemmon, Tony Curtis, and Marilyn Monroe, is perhaps the best-known of the movies shot at the Del. Some of the Del's other screen credits, however, were not so highly acclaimed, including a short-lived and entirely forgettable parapsychology show starring the late Sebastian Cabot. The in-room televisions at the Del have a channel devoted exclusively to screening the many films and programs made on the premises.

A taped tour, available for rent at the hotel's front desk, introduces visitors to the Del's rich history and many curiosities, which include the sugar pine–covered Crown Room, believed to be the largest support-free room in the world, and the hotel's three elevators, which are the oldest lifts still in operation anywhere. The beach behind the hotel—one of the nicest in the county—is open to the public. Call 435-6611 for more information.

As Orange Avenue continues beyond the Hotel del Coronado, it passes by several tall condominiums. When John Spreckels bought the Del, shortly after it was built, the crafty businessman erected cottages, tents, dance halls, a casino, an indoor swimming pool, and even a Japanese tea garden on this 24-acre site to cater to locals who liked his sprawling hotel but couldn't afford his room rates. For many years afterward, this area, known as Tent City, was a favorite summer vacation spot for San Diegans, who appreciated the resort's reasonable rates and its proximity to the glitzy Del. Today ten 17-story condominiums occupy the site. When they were built in the late 1960s, these high-rises caused quite a controversy, helping galvanize local voters into supporting the creation of the California Coastal Commission, the state-run organization which today controls all construction on the California coastline.

Below the Hotel del Coronado, and just north of Silver Strand State Park, is the U.S. Naval Amphibious Base, the West Coast headquarters for the U.S. Navy's SEAL teams. The members of this elite unit are legendary warriors who have earned their reputation for no-holds-barred heroism in every conflict since World War II. Unfortunately, many Americans know of this courageous unit only because of its use of specially trained dolphins in underwater demolition missions, a practice which has been criticized by environmentalist groups.

To join the SEALs, recruits undergo a punishing boot camp known as "Hell Week." During just one day of this grueling seven-day exercise, would-be SEALs are brought to an isolated beach, where they are forced to sit in the water Indian-style, with their backs to the surf. There they remain, for 24 hours, while wave after wave crashes against their naked bodies. An attending physician monitors vital signs, and when a recruit begins to lapse into hypothermia or unconsciousness (not an uncommon occurrence) he's escorted toward a nearby fire—close enough to see and hear its crackling glow but too far away to feel it. When the recruit's vital signs naturally return to a near-normal state, he's escorted back to the shoreline, where the grueling test continues.

For a closer look at Coronado's many attractions, consider one of the tours conducted by the Coronado Historical Society. The tours depart each Tuesday, Wednesday, and Thursday from the Glorietta Bay Inn, across the street from the Hotel del Coronado. The cost is $4 per person and reservations are not required. The 90-minute tour includes a peek inside the Hotel del Coronado (including a look at the Pinewood Cottage, one of the three Coronado homes where the Duchess of Windsor lived); the John Spreckels mansion, built in 1903; the home where Frank Baum wrote *The Wizard of Oz*; and other points of interest. For information about these tours, call 435-5993 or 435-5892.

Imperial Beach
and the Tijuana Slough
National Wildlife Refuge

The ten-mile-long Silver Strand connects upscale Coronado to its neighbor to the south, the decidedly downmarket town of Imperial Beach. Although it's one of the smallest cities in San Diego County, just 4.5 square miles, Imperial Beach has enormous problems. For starters, it has no tax base. For years, residents have balked at any talk of a local levy—even one that would pay for essential emergency services—and politicians who have challenged this sentiment have found themselves out of a job. The absence of municipal services gives Imperial Beach a shabby, lawless flavor, and the fact the town is located alongside one of the major routes for illegal immigration and drug smuggling into the U.S. only adds to this problem. What's more, the sewage-filled Tijuana River flows out of Mexico and through Imperial Beach, where it empties into the ocean. As a result, it's impossible to transform Imperial Beach into a seaside resort like Coronado, even though that would be a lucrative source of revenue for the cash-strapped city.

But Imperial Beach has its attractions, not the least of which is its unobstructed views of the sights in neighboring Mexico, including Tijuana's impressive Bullring by the Sea, and Las Islas de los Coronados. Border Field State Park, just south of town, is the only beach in the county where horseback riding is permitted.

Imperial Beach is also home to the Tijuana Slough National Wildlife Refuge, the largest surviving wetland in Southern California. Hundreds of species thrive in the reserve's 2,500 acres, including the endangered peregrine falcon, brown pelican, and clapper rail. Located along the spring-fall migration route for hundreds of exotic species, the reserve is a birdwatcher's delight. The visitor center, run by the U.S. Fish and Wildlife Service, has information on the other animals and plants in the sanctuary, and offers free guided tours on the first two Saturdays of each month. Call 575-1290 for more information.

Chapter Seven
◆ ◆ ◆ ◆ ◆ ◆ ◆ ◆ ◆ ◆ ◆

High Points and Hot Spots

S AN DIEGO'S back country—the 2,000-square-mile expanse of foothills, highland meadows, mountains, and deserts that begins about twenty miles southeast of downtown—is a place of staggering beauty and breathtaking variety. Unfortunately, many visitors, and even many long-time residents, don't take the time to explore this vast and varied region, overlooking what is arguably San Diego's finest attraction.

During most of the eighteenth and nineteenth centuries, the back country was a refuge for the Kumeyaay, who drifted back into the region in increasing numbers as the Spaniards and Americans took over the tribe's coastal homelands. The Spaniards considered the Indians' eastward exodus cowardly, and called one of the more remote Indian settlements *El Valle de las Viejas* (Span., Valley of the Old Women).

But the urge to return was natural. The mountains here were part of the Kumeyaay's ancestral lands and they played an important role in the tribe's cosmology. One Kumeyaay legend explained why three mountains near

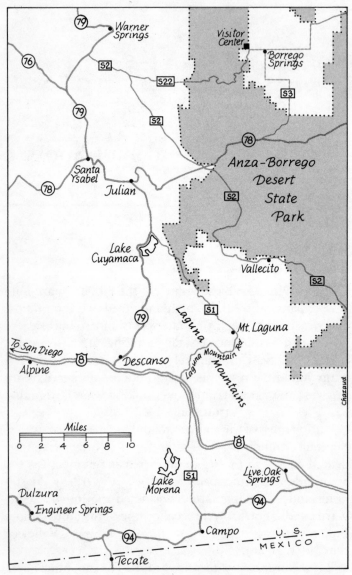

Mountains and Desert

Lake Cuyamaca were clustered together while a fourth, known as Pine Tree Mountain, stood alone to the south. According to the tale, the four mountains were constantly bickering, and Pine Tree Mountain grew so tired of the fracases that it finally moved to get some peace. Another legend told how Fanita, the daughter of Chief Cuyamaca, carried her stricken lover, Carissa, to these mountains, where she brought him back from the dead with water from a spring near Lake Morena. Yet another tale referred to one of the mountains here as *E-yee* (Kumeyaay, nest) because it was believed animals eluded hunters and death by fleeing to a secret nest or den hidden on its slopes. The back country was also the domain of the eagle and the bear, two animals highly esteemed by the Kumeyaay, and so the whole area was thought of as a sacred, magical place.

Modern visitors can catch a glimpse of the magic by taking Interstate 8 east to the lookout point at *In-ko-Pah* (Kumeyaay, Mountain People), which overlooks the neighboring Imperial Valley and offers stunning views of the desert floor, the Salton Sea, and the Chocolate Mountains beyond. An even more impressive view can be had at Desert View, on Laguna Mountain, where the picture-perfect desert panorama is framed by the surrounding oak and pine forest.

During the early years of the American period, employees of the ill-fated San Diego and Gila Railroad battled steep grades, rocky terrain, and Mexican and Indian outlaws as they worked in the back country to carve a direct rail link to the East. The company's engineers finally abandoned the project when they realized that even if they managed to get to the top of the mountains, they would need to clear four 4,000-foot crests on the way down. Engineer Springs, a small well southeast of Dulzura (Span., sweetness) on state Route 94, marks the spot where some of these workers camped.

In the end, it was the indefatigable John Spreckels who finally established a rail connection to the cities of the East. But his San Diego and Arizona Eastern Railroad, built in 1916 at a cost of over $18 million, never conquered San Diego's back country grades. Instead, the tracks ran through Mexico, from Tijuana to Tecate, and reentered the U.S. near Campo (Span., field), passing through the only international railway tunnel that runs into or out of the U.S. Spreckels's railroad survived until 1976, when a hurricane destroyed many of the line's trestles and bridges and put it out of business.

Today, both Interstate 8 and state Route 94 provide good access to the back country area. But getting to some of the spots described in this chapter, including Julian and Borrego Springs, may require taking secondary routes (see the map on page 114).

If you plan to hike or camp in the back country, take the usual precautions. Most problems can be avoided by using common sense. Some back country areas receive four times the precipitation the rest of the county gets— as much as forty inches anually. You should be prepared for sudden changes in the weather, particularly during the winter, when storm fronts can move in and drop a deep blanket of snow in the higher elevations. If you go into the desert, take a map, at least two quarts of water per person, plenty of sunscreen, a hat, and sturdy shoes. Poison oak is a problem in the higher elevations. Western rattlesnakes and Colorado desert sidewinders are common in both the mountains and desert, though they remain out of sight during the daylight hours. If you see either of these poisonous snakes, contact a ranger to have it removed to a remote location. Taking native plants or animals, Indian artifacts, fossils, or rocks from state or federal parks is prohibited. And please remember to pick up after yourself. Disposing of your trash properly, even if it means hauling it back to your house or hotel room, keeps the back country beautiful.

Mount Laguna

Mount Laguna is located about sixty miles east of downtown San Diego, just off the Sunrise Highway in one of the few wooded sections of Cleveland National Forest. It has towering oak and pine trees and panoramic views of the desert floor, over six thousand feet below.

Although Mount Laguna is open year-round, the best time to explore is during the summer and fall. The park is extremely popular during the winter—especially after storms, when families bring their children up to play in the snow. Unfortunately, few Southern Californians know how to drive in the white stuff and these winding mountain roads are the last place you want to run into an unseasoned amateur. Only the truly daring are encouraged to drive up Mount Laguna after a winter storm. If you decide to visit after a snowfall, remember to bring tire chains; the California Highway Patrol permits only chain-equipped vehicles on the steep road up to the mountain's crest.

There are a number of trails on Mount Laguna (including a section of the Pacific Crest Trail, which runs from Mexico to Canada), but two are especially worthwhile. The Wooded Hill Trail, on the west side of the Sunrise Highway, is a well-marked footpath that climbs through Mount Laguna's alpine meadows and chaparral thickets. The trail ends at the park's highest point and offers views, on clear days, of San Diego and the Pacific beyond. The less strenuous mile-long Desert Rim Trail, which originates at the Burnt Rancheria Campground, just east of the Sunrise Highway, is a cactus-lined path that hugs the eastern cliffs of Mount Laguna and overlooks the desert floor, the old Butterfield Stage station in Vallecito, and Agua Caliente County Park, one of three mineral hot springs in the area. Information on both trails is available from the ranger station, located beside the general store.

Mount Laguna is home to many wild species. Regular visitors have reported seeing mule deer, bobcats, coyotes, and even the rare mountain lion. Among the birds you can see at Mount Laguna are scrub jays, band-tailed pigeons, chickadees, nuthatches, Steller's jays, woodpeckers, titmice, ravens, hummingbirds, and various hawks.

Lake Cuyamaca

The Spanish called this mountain lake *La Laguna Que Se Seca* (Span., the lake that dries up), because its water levels drop precipitously during hot dry summers. The Kumeyaay knew it as *Cuyamaca* (Kumeyaay, rain above)—the name it goes by today. In drought years Cuyamaca can be a pitiful thing to behold. But in years with average to above-average rainfall it is full and stocked with fish.

Cuyamaca first became important toward the end of the nineteenth century, when it was one of the lakes looked to by thirsty San Diegans to help solve the city's water problems. Today, San Diego imports ninety percent of its water from outside the county, but in its early days the city relied solely on local rainfall to satisfy its needs. As San Diego began to grow during the 1880s, spreading out over the dry mesas, rainfall was no longer able to slake the local thirst. Engineers turned to the back country's many watersheds to augment the city's water supply.

The first attempt to tap the mountain lakes came in 1889, when the San Diego Flume Company began pumping the waters of Lake Cuyamaca to San Diego via a 35-

mile wooden duct, which ran alongside the banks of the San Diego River and then fed into the city's mains. When the flume opened in February 1889, there was an enormous celebration in San Diego. A giant parade ended at a hydrant where the water was to be tasted for the first time. When the hydrant was opened, water shot a hundred feet into the air and local papers reported that enthusiastic citizens praised the "excellent taste of the new water." Actually, the "new water" was the same water locals had been drinking for years: The water from Cuyamaca was still working its way through air-bound pipes east of the city and wouldn't reach San Diego for another three weeks. The water shooting skyward came from an artesian well near Balboa Park. The owners and operators of the well, the San Diego Water Company, put aside their rivalry for the day and pumped water into the San Diego Flume Company's pipes.

Although its debut was nothing to gush about, Lake Cuyamaca came to play an important role in San Diego's water supply system. But as the city continued to grow, its water problem worsened. A drought in 1916 created a crisis. In desperation, the city turned to Charles Hatfield, a self-styled "rainmaker," who promised to end the city's water problems—for $10,000. With no other option presenting itself, the city council accepted the offer and Hatfield went to work.

Near Lake Morena, just south of Pine Valley, Hatfield erected a number of curious towers, which he called "precipitation plants." On top of the towers he placed open bins containing some apparently potent rainmaking chemicals. Within weeks, clouds were gathering and the first drops began falling. The drops became a downpour, which became a deluge, which finally became a full-scale disaster. And then, they say, it *really* rained. Over 16 inches fell within the space of two days. The Morena Dam, which had been almost empty, came within 18 inches of its 22-billion-gallon capacity. The dam at Lower Otay burst, causing calamitous floods and many deaths. In San Ysidro, the Tijuana River rose over its banks, washing the utopian dreams of the "Little Landers" out to sea.

When Hatfield demanded payment for services rendered, the city came back with an offer of its own, saying it would pay his tab only if he assumed liability for the $4 million in lawsuits brought against the city for damage caused by the floods. After considering a suit against the city, Hatfield thought better and departed the city without collecting—or paying—a dime. Although Hatfield regarded the San Diego project as one of his finest rainmaking accomplishments, he later surpassed himself, reportedly producing over forty inches of rain in three hours near Randsburg in the Mojave Desert.

Today, the 21,000-acre park surrounding Lake Cuyamaca has trails, campsites, and paths for horseback riding. The county stocks the lake with trout, and anglers are welcome. The park's Indian Museum and headquarters are open from 8 to 5 weekdays, and from approximately 10 to 2 on weekends (the times vary because the volunteers who run the museum don't always arrive on time). A map detailing the park's offerings is available for a nominal fee. Call 765-0755 for more information.

Julian and Santa Ysabel

Julian, which got its start as a mining town in the nineteenth century, is located about ten miles northwest of Lake Cuyamaca, in a high mountain meadow surrounded by orchards and stands of pine trees. A popular weekend retreat for city-weary San Diegans seeking old-fashioned charm, Julian is known primarily for its apples. During the city's annual Apple Festival in October, the townspeople go mad for the fruit, selling ciders, pies, jams, and more, much of it produced from locally grown apples. Accommodations, always tight in Julian, are almost impossible to come by during the event, so you should make your lodging plans well in advance.

During the 1870s, it was gold rather than apples that drove the locals mad. In 1869, placer gold was discovered in the hills outside Julian. As word of the strike spread, prospectors from all over the country poured into the area. By all accounts, the sleepy community of Julian was quickly transformed into a passable version of Sodom, as gamblers, would-be tycoons, prostitutes, outlaws, confidence men, and sundry other predatory types converged on the town. In the first year alone, over seventy men drank themselves to death. The surrounding countryside became one huge open pit as hundreds of prospectors dug mines and then abandoned them on a whim or a hunch. By 1880, most of the gold had been extracted from the area. Many of the prospectors packed up their belongings and headed to Tombstone, Arizona, where a new gold rush was under way.

Some diehards continued to work in the isolated hills around Julian into the 1930s. By the time the last one had given up, an estimated $15 million worth of gold had been removed from the area. The Eagle Mining Company, at the north end of C Street, provides sightseers with an opportunity to step back into Julian's gilded age, with 1½-hour guided tours of an old gold mine. Call 765-0036 for more information.

In a stunning valley five miles northwest of Julian is Santa Ysabel, the small town where the Franciscans opened an *asistencia* in 1818 to minister to the back country Indians. Today, the major attraction is Dudley's Bakery, a family-run outfit justly famous for its wonderful variety of breads, including a spicy jalapeño bread and a unique cheese bread. The original *asistencia*, rebuilt in 1924, is about two miles north of the bakery, on state

Route 78, next to *El Campo Santo* (Span., the cemetery), an Indian burial ground in use since 1820. Years ago, Indians gathered at this cemetery twice a year to celebrate the *Fiesta de las Cruces* (Span., festival of the crosses), singing ancient songs and swapping old tales, but these events have not taken place for some time. A memorial in the cemetery honors the Indian veterans of World War I, World War II, and the Vietnam War. The small museum on the premises exhibits artifacts and photos of the local Indian bands. A $1 donation is suggested for admission. Be sure to turn off the lights when you leave. Picnic tables are also available, but dogs are not allowed on the premises.

Campo

Campo is near the eastern terminus of state Route 94, a little-traveled road today but once the most important east-west thoroughfare in the southern section of the county. Because the town was originally settled by pioneers from the Lone Star State, who found this desolate, windswept patch of scrub somehow homey, Campo was known for many years as Little Texas or New Texas.

These days, the main attraction in Campo is the Mountain Empire Historical Society's headquarters, housed in a nineteenth-century dry-goods store originally owned by Silas and Lumen Gaskill, two brothers who moved into the area in the 1850s. This imposing two-story building, with its four-foot-thick walls, was actually the Gaskill brothers' second store—constructed after they had a spot of trouble. Their first was a wooden clapboard affair, built over a mountain stream; the Gaskills preserved perishable items by lowering them into the cool waters below through a trap door inside.

As it turned out, that trap door preserved more than

eggs and milk. In 1875, the Gaskill brothers' store was the site of one of the bloodiest shootouts in the Wild West—more deadly, some reckon, than the more famous Gunfight at the OK Corral. Six Mexican outlaws attacked the store, opening fire and hitting one of the Gaskill brothers in the chest. Though wounded, he crawled back into the store, dropped down into the creek through the trap door, and returned fire from behind some rocks, drawing the attention of other residents in town. Two Mexicans were killed in the crossfire and the remaining four either died of wounds received in the gun battle, or were captured and hanged—it depends on who you believe. A diorama in the museum depicts these events, and each year, on Memorial Day weekend, the gunfight is reenacted by townspeople dressed in period outfits.

The Mountain Empire Historical Society's museum also has a collection of army memorabilia dating from World War II, when over five thousand troops, many of them members of segregated black cavalry units, were stationed at Campo's Camp Lockett, which was built to defend California from a Japanese invasion through Mexico.

The Pacific Southwest Railroad Museum is just north of Campo. The restored steam locomotives and passenger cars at the museum are interesting enough, but the weekend train rides, which take passengers on a 16-mile trek through the hills around Campo, are especially worthwhile. The museum is open Saturday and Sunday from 10 to 5. Call 697-7762 for more information.

Opposite Campo, in a picturesque valley on the Mexican side of the border, is Tecate, a small and friendly town famous for its brewery and cattle ranches. Tecate dates back to the 1830s, when the area was part of a grant made by the Mexican government to Señor Don Juan Bandini, who repaid this faith in dubious fashion, by giving aid and comfort to the American conquerors.

Borrego Springs and Anza-Borrego Desert State Park

Borrego Springs, San Diego's splendid desert resort, is located about twenty-five miles northeast of Julian, in a bowl-shaped basin at the foot of the San Ysidro Mountains. The *Borrego* (Span., yearling lamb) in the town's name comes from the majestic bighorn sheep that roam the surrounding boulder-strewn hills. The "Springs" comes from the deep wells underneath the desert floor. The wells contain enough water to permit Borrego Springs to avoid the strict water rationing that is mandatory in the rest of Southern California during times of drought.

Borrego Springs is bounded on all sides by the 600,000-acre Anza-Borrego Desert State Park, the largest state park in the West. The park's Visitor Center, located at the west end of Palm Canyon Drive, is a good place to start your tour. Open daily from 9 to 5 from October to May, and on Saturdays and Sundays from 10 to 3 during the hot summer months, the center presents a must-see slide show, which provides an introduction to the park's many points of interest. Call 767-4684 for more information.

One of the best trails in the park is the 1 1/2-mile Palm Canyon Trail. It begins at one end of the Borrego Palm Canyon Campground and follows a moderate incline up the side of a canyon to a palm-ringed oasis at the trail's end. The trees at the oasis are California fan palms (*Washingtonia filifera*), the only palm tree native to California.

The Panoramic Overlook Trail, which also begins at the Borrego Palm Canyon Campground, is a more challenging trek, but the view of the surrounding countryside from its crest is worth the extra effort.

Visitors who expect the desert to be little more than a bleak, desolate patch of sand will find Borrego a pleasant surprise. There are miles of flat, scrub-covered desert floor to be sure, but there are also deep canyons, wide washes, and the dramatic Borrego Badlands, making the area a place of infinite variety. For visitors used to urban congestion and suburban sprawl, the desert's overwhelming silence and vast emptiness can be moving. A visit to Font's Point, which overlooks the miles of wind- and rain-carved ravines known as the Borrego Badlands, is especially breathtaking, providing the sightseer with a glimpse of a part of the desert that can't be seen from the highway.

A good time to visit the area is between October and May, when temperatures are below 100°. During those months, the townspeople of Borrego Springs host a number of celebrations, including the annual Grapefruit Festival in April. (December through April are the best months for buying locally grown grapefruit.) In March and April the wildflowers, cholla cacti, ocotillo, and agave are at their flowering peak. In the more remote areas of the park, bobcats, coyotes, and bighorn sheep are occasionally seen; roadrunners, jackrabbits, quail, and a dozen different reptiles and amphibians are apt to pop up anywhere. A "scorecard" for visitors, highlighting the plants and animals of the park, is available from the park headquarters for a nominal fee. The park also publishes a daily calendar of events, listing ranger- and volunteer-led tours and events which are, with very few exceptions, free and worth investigating.

Scientists have uncovered the fossil remains of a giant ground sloth, an 18-foot-tall camel, a rhinoceros, and an imperial mammoth around Borrego Springs. These finds suggest that the area was once a tropical rain forest on the edge of the Gulf of California. The best guess is that the lush landscape gave way to the desert you see today about fifteen thousand years ago, and that the California fan palms found throughout Anza-Borrego Desert State Park are the only relic of those prehistoric days.

The original human inhabitants of the Borrego Valley

were the Cahuilla people, members of the Shoshonean family, who settled in the area six thousand years ago. In 1774, Juan Baptista de Anza, a Spanish explorer, led the first European expedition through the area, as he searched for an overland route to California. During the late eighteenth century and through the nineteenth century, Mexican trappers and American pioneers regularly used de Anza's trail between Yuma (in what is now Arizona) and Los Angeles; the route came to be called the Southern Emigrant Trail. Most of these adventurers passed through Borrego Springs without leaving a mark. Others will never be forgotten.

In 1829, a colorful character named Thomas L. "Peg Leg" Smith wandered down the Southern Emigrant Trail on his way to California. Arriving in Los Angeles, Peg Leg produced some rocks he said he'd picked up near Borrego Springs. Local metallurgists told him the rocks were pure gold. At least that's what Peg Leg said they said. For one dubious reason or another, Peg Leg put off returning to Borrego Springs for almost twenty years; when he finally did come back, in 1850—with financial backers in tow—he had great difficulty rediscovering his "lost" mine. Peg Leg stuck around Borrego Springs until he died in 1866, searching the mountains by day and spinning fantastic yarns by night. Today, Smith is remembered by the townspeople of Borrego Springs, who hold the "Peg Leg Smith Liar's Contest" on the first Saturday in April each year, at the "Peg Leg Monument" on county road S22.

In later years, the Southern Emigrant Road was used by the Butterfield Overland Stage Company, which was authorized by Congress to carry mail from St. Louis to San Francisco. The line carried passengers as well, but the journey offered few opportunities for sightseeing in the modern sense. Among other things, passengers were required to arm themselves for the trip and were expected to defend the stage against Indian and outlaw attacks. When the terrain made travel difficult, as it did in the Box Canyon area outside Borrego Springs, passengers were obliged to get out and push.

South of Borrego Springs on S2, the county road that roughly follows the old Southern Emigrant Trail, is Vallecito, the last desert station on the Butterfield Overland Stage Company's western route. Today, the stage station has been reconstructed and is open to the public. Agua Caliente Hot Springs, a county park with natural hot-water baths, is three miles south of Vallecito.

Anza-Borrego Desert State Park is one of the few parks in California where open camping is permitted. Some spots charge no fee whatsoever, but even the most popular campgrounds cost less than $20 a night during peak season (December 1 to April 30). Primitive campsites, many of which are located miles from park headquarters, are usually available, but reservations are suggested for the Borrego Palm Canyon Campground and Tamarisk Grove Campground, which offer restrooms, showers, shade ramadas, and campfire programs. Call 1-800-444-7275 for reservations.

Chapter Eight

••••••••••

Mexico

NO VISIT to San Diego is complete without a trip into neighboring Mexico, where the romance and adventure of Old California are still very much alive.

A daylong excursion to Tijuana, Rosarito, Ensenada, or Tecate—the principal cities on the northern tip of *Baja* (Span., lower) California—will give you a chance to check out the local color, browse for pottery, leather, or silver bargains (and haggle with the merchants over prices), take in the action at the local jai alai fronton or bullfight arena, and enjoy a margarita at a restaurant that might just change the way you think about Mexican food. And if you leave early, you can make it back to San Diego in time for a sunset dinner overlooking the Pacific.

Unpredictable gas supplies, hairpin highway turns, arcane insurance regulations, and unfamiliar local geography conspire to make motoring in Mexico a dangerous proposition for the first-time tourist. Frequent visitors to Tijuana, especially, avoid driving because of the lines—often an hour long on weekdays and even longer on weekends and holidays—to get back into the U.S. Your best bet is to get yourself down to the international border by car, bus, taxi, or San Diego Trolley ($1.50 each way for kids and adults; 60 cents for seniors), and then to cross over into Tijuana on foot. The shopping, dining, and gaming options on Avenida Revolución and Paseo de los Heroes are then just fifteen minutes away on foot or five minutes away by the famed Tijuana taxi.

Greyhound, Mexicoach, and a number of local bus companies offer hassle-free service from hotels throughout San Diego to the heart of Tijuana.

Ensenada, the bustling port city about sixty miles south of the border, is connected to Tijuana by a fairly modern toll road, which hugs the peninsula's spectacular coastline and passes through the resort towns of Rosarito and Calafia and the delightful fishing village of Puerto Nuevo. The tolls between Tijuana and Ensenada run around $7 each way. Another way to reach Ensenada is aboard one of the cruise ships that leave from the Cruise Ship Terminal in San Diego. The Pacific Star Line, for example, offers a daily cruise to Ensenada; passage, which runs $89 per person on weekdays and $99 on weekends, includes three buffet-style meals and admission to the ship's casino. Visitors who want more than just a quick glimpse of Mexico, however, are advised to consider another option, because most of the Pacific Star's 13-hour cruise is spent at sea and passengers are lucky to get more than three hours in Mexico.

Getting to Tecate, the inland town famous for its shaded central plaza, its brewery, and its friendly residents, is simpler and cheaper. Just take state Route 94 east, through Lemon Grove, Spring Valley, Jamul, and Engineer Springs, to state Route 188 south. Two minutes later, you'll be in Tecate. The lines at the border are shorter here.

Although a day trip to Mexico requires no passport or visa, you will need a tourist card if you are going to be in

Baja for 72 hours or more. Stop by the Mexican Consulate General's office at 610 A Street in downtown San Diego (231-8414) to pick up one of these free documents and to get any last-minute information you need about your trip. If you're visiting for the first time, stop by the Tijuana Tourism and Convention Bureau's kiosk just across the border, or on the corner of *Calle 1* (Span., First Avenue) and Avenida Revolución in Tijuana, for more information on Tijuana's offerings.

Keep in mind that you will have a much better time in Mexico if you use common courtesy and common sense (see also pages 41–43). Like any city of its size, Tijuana has its share of pickpockets, con men, and assorted operators looking to prey on naive visitors. You should remember also that while Baja *norte* is a free-trade zone its residents haven't completely taken leave of their senses: There are many good bargains to be had down here, but deals that sound too good to be true probably are.

Be especially wary of real-estate offerings. The Treaty of Guadalupe Hidalgo, which ended the Mexican-American War and ceded California, Arizona, Texas, New Mexico, Nevada, Utah, and portions of Colorado and Wyoming to the United States, created a lot of resentment toward *Yanquis* (Span. slang, Americans) and forged an intense commitment to Mexico's territorial integrity. As a result, there are laws that bar non-Mexicans from owning any land within 50 kilometers of the coast or within 100 kilometers of the border. Although the present government is beginning to introduce free-market principles that will attract much-needed foreign investment, there are still many potential drawbacks and pitfalls. Americans do "own" vacation homes across the border, but the smart ones contacted an attorney first.

If you decide to drive down to Rosarito or Ensenada, stay alert and cruise at or slightly below the posted speed limit. At night, the dangers increase dramatically on Mex-

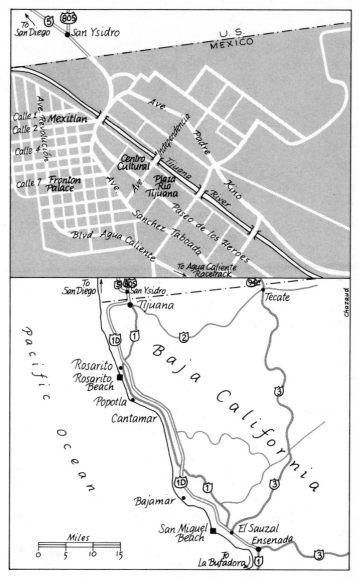

Tijuana (above) and Northern Baja California (below)

ico's roads, especially in the rural areas outside Tijuana. If you're south of the city after dark, find a hotel or motel, check in, and relax. You will avoid the assorted hazards that make night driving here unpredictable and unrecommended.

Tijuana

For much of its history, Tijuana was a rough-and-tumble Sin City, a place where rubes, rowdies, and roughnecks from San Diego and all points north came for bad women, cheap curios, and any booze they could lay their hands on. During Prohibition, when the manufacture, transportation, and sale of intoxicating liquors was banned in the U.S., Tijuana was the first spot south of Vancouver where residents of the West Coast could slake their thirst for alcohol. Not surprisingly, the city did a brisk business. Unfortunately, some local businessmen didn't know where to draw the line and the city quickly became notorious for its willingness to satisfy—for a price—any other tastes that might be banned elsewhere. Gambling, legalized here during the 1920s, attracted celebrities like W.C. Fields and Charlie Chaplin, but the veneer provided by these occasional visits from Hollywood's aristocracy barely concealed the lurid, low-rent reality of the city's sprawling Zona Rosa (Span., red-light district). With repeal, the bars and brothels of Tijuana sank deeper still, showcasing perversions designed to titillate the underage Navy enlisted men and bored high-school juniors who still bothered to visit. By the early 1970s, Tijuana was an international embarrassment.

Thankfully, much of that has changed. Today, Tijuana has the highest per capita income in Mexico and is the country's fourth largest metropolitan area, with over one million inhabitants. The growth and prosperity have been the result of political reform and economic diversification, which began haltingly after gambling was outlawed in the mid-1930s. More recent development has brought scores of new restaurants, hotels, stores, and festive watering holes to town, as well as a number of worthwhile attractions like the Centro Cultural, Tijuana's sleek, modern museum complex, located in the *Zona Rio* (Span., river zone), a neighborhood bordering the Tijuana River that has really prospered as the city has redefined itself.

The natural place to begin any visit is on Avenida Revolución, the city's main tourist thoroughfare, where the sparkling designer boutiques, discos, and restaurants of the new Tijuana jostle with the few lingering reminders of the city's bad old days.

You might start at the Fronton Palace, at Avenida Revolución and Calle 7, where spectators wager on jai alai, a two-man racquetball-like game reputed to be the fastest sport on earth. General admission is $3; box seats and courtside tables are $5. Visitors interested in other types of gaming can check out Agua Caliente Racetrack, south on Avenida Revolución (it becomes Bulevar Agua Caliente), which features horseracing on weekend afternoons and dog racing on weekend evenings. If you're not squeamish about your sports, consider a visit to Tijuana's spectacular Plaza de Toros Monumental, located by the sea about 5 miles west of the downtown area, where bullfights are held every Sunday afternoon from May through September.

Of course shopping is the real game in Tijuana. The stores on Avenida Revolución offer everything from handcrafted crystal, pottery, and glass items to imported French perfumes and upscale fashions, discounted 10 to 25 percent. There's a Ralph Lauren shop adjacent to the Fronton Palace, a Guess outlet further north on Revolución, and a brand new Hard Rock Cafe, occupying a spot on the northernmost end of the street. Sara's and Maxim's, two upscale department stores with high-quality items, cater to both tourists and well-heeled locals.

Just one block off Revolución is Mexitlan. Part theme park, part cultural exhibit, Mexitlan is a collection of miniature models of Mexico's architectural landmarks. It's open 24 hours a day. Each of Mexico's states is represented at Mexitlan, and a trip here, along with a visit to the Centro Cultural in the Zona Rio, gives the first-time visitor a nice introduction to the country's rich history and culture.

One of the exasperating joys of shopping in Tijuana is the custom, widely accepted on Avenida Revolución, of dickering over prices. It's a joy because it turns shopping into a game; it's exasperating because, as it turns out, the merchants are better at it than you are. You're encouraged to test your bargaining skills, but before you turn blue in the face trying to do the impossible, remember that prices are only negotiable in the smaller souvenir stores, which sell items produced in Mexico. Retailers selling imported goods—like the shops in the impressive glass-and-steel Drug Store, on the corner of Calle 4 and Avenida Revolución—don't deviate from marked prices. And for good reason: In many cases, Mexican merchants face steep fines if they offer unauthorized discounts, particularly on imported items.

If you build up a thirst haggling with the merchants, there are a number of worthwhile watering holes close by on Avenida Revolución, including Tia Juana Tilly's (adjacent to the Fronton Palace), Margarita Village, the infamous Long Bar, and, of course, the new Hard Rock Cafe. Pop into the one where the noise and festivity levels match your mood. There are also a number of very good restaurants here, including La Costa, Tia Juana Tilly's, Chiki Jai, Bol Corona, and Cafe La Especial. (See pages 157–158 for more information on these restaurants.)

Caesar's restaurant and hotel, said to be the place where the Caesar salad was invented, is located on the corner of Avenida Revolución and Calle 5. Unfortunately, its culinary moment has passed, and the restaurant can't be recommended.

Other parts of Tijuana, particularly Paseo de los Heroes in the Zona Rio, have undergone intense redevelopment and now attract local shoppers and tourists with their stores and bars. Plaza Rio Tijuana, at the corner of Paseo de los Heroes and Avenida Independencia, is a standout, drawing a binational group of browsers and buyers with department stores like Sears and Dorian's, specialty shops, custom-leather stores, and restaurants. Pueblo Amigo, another mall on Paseo de los Heroes, is also becoming quite popular. Shoe lovers should visit the Plaza de Zapato, a fifty-store mall in the Zona Rio that sells nothing but designer footwear from around the world.

When night falls and the stores close (most merchants in Tijuana are open for business from 10 A.M. to 7 P.M.— with some stores closing between 2 and 4 in the afternoon for siesta), Paseo de los Heroes is transformed into night-club row. Some of Tijuana's hottest youth-oriented night-clubs, including Club Oh!, Iguanas, and the cavernous Baby Rock, are located here.

Rosarito Beach

Rosarito, the small town about twenty miles south of Tijuana, just off the toll road, is known primarily for its resort, the Rosarito Beach Hotel. Indeed for much of the present century, there was little here *but* the resort. The first settlement in the area was established in the late 1750s, when Jesuit priests established a small mission, *La Mision San Borja*, in a remote patch of desert about thirty-five miles east of present-day Rosarito. When the King of Spain expelled the Jesuits from the New World in early

1760s, the mission was abandoned and Rosarito returned to its natural state until 1926, when the hotel was built overlooking the vast beach below.

Today, that beach is a favorite with surfers, body surfers, and horseback riders, and the Rosarito Beach Hotel is getting a run for its money as more and more inns and condominium projects pop up in the area to take advantage of the tourism boom and the town's spectacular setting. Calafia, about six miles south of Rosarito, is gaining favor as a weekend getaway spot for crowd-weary Californians. The views from the windswept rocks here are magnificent, capturing the splendid isolation and sinister silence of Baja *norte*.

Puerto Nuevo, the next town along the toll road, is a former fishing village that has gained regional fame for its lobster meals, prepared and served by the wives of the local fishermen. If you venture down to Ensenada without stopping here, you're breaking a visitor tradition at least twenty-five years old. Ensenada has good restaurants, it's true (including many famed for their abalone), but no one does lobster quite like the women of Puerto Nuevo.

Ensenada

Ensenada, a seaport city sixty miles below the border, is about as far south as the first-timer can venture on a day trip.

Although shipping is Ensenada's principal form of commerce, the city offers the same haggling and bargain adventures of Tijuana without all the congestion associated with that city. Wine aficionados should note that Ensenada is also the center of Mexico's wine country, responsible for 75 percent of all the wine and brandy produced in the country. The Santo Tomás Winery, founded by the Dominicans in the nineteenth century, offers daily tours and tastings at 666 Avenida Miramar.

Most of the shops, restaurants, and hotels in Ensenada are located near the city's central harbor, *Bahia Todos Santos*, (Span., All Saints Bay), named by Sebastián Vizcaíno, the same explorer who gave San Diego its name. The main drag is Avenida Lopez Mateos, just east of the waterfront, where merchants sell baskets, pottery, and leather. Avenida Ruiz is home to a number of rowdy honky-tonks, including Hussong's Cantina, the world-famous saloon that has been drawing hard-playing tourists since it was founded by a German immigrant in 1892. Fans of the unusual should take a quick drive into Cañon Guadalupe, a farming valley just outside Ensenada which originally was settled by refugees fleeing Lenin's revolution in Russia. The blond-haired, blue-eyed descendants of these early residents—sporting names like Poppoff and Dimytriw but speaking flawless Spanish—continue to be a prominent part of the valley's population seventy years later.

With a climate and setting not unlike San Diego's, Ensenada is a popular destination for sportsmen. Each spring, Ensenada serves as the finish line for two sporting events of note. In early April, the Rosarito-to-Ensenada bike ride closes the inland road linking the two cities, as thousands of biking enthusiasts make the fifty-mile trek. In early May, yachtsmen compete in the annual Newport-to-Ensenada Yacht Race. Sportfishing is also very big down here; yellowtail is the fish of choice, found in abundance in the azure waters offshore. The best beaches in the area are located just above and just below the city. San Miguel, eight miles north of Ensenada, is a very popular surfing spot. Estero Beach, just south of town, is favored by swimmers, although currents here can be treacherous during high tide. When the tide rises, get out of the water and head to *La Bufadora* (Span., the snort), a spectacular tidal blowhole, located about twenty-five minutes south of downtown, which shoots water as much as a hundred feet into the air. On your way back to the U.S., stop by Riviera del Pacifico, the sprawling oceanfront center built during the 1930s as a casino by Jack Dempsey.

Tecate

Tecate, nestled in an agricultural valley thirty miles southeast of San Diego (off state Route 94), is the least touristy of the border cities. Surrounded by sprawling cattle ranches, Tecate has never been a rowdy, raunchy place like Tijuana. The town's secret may be the border crossing, which is open only from 6 A.M. to midnight—creating a de facto curfew. Then again, it could be Tecate's "hot" reputation: During the summer, it's not unusual for the city to be twenty degrees warmer than Tijuana and a blistering thirty degrees warmer than Ensenada.

Whatever it is, it keeps the crowds away. That's just fine with the dedicated fans of the city, who come back again and again to enjoy Tecate's uncomplicated pleasures. The routine of these repeat visitors is as simple as the city's charms, and first-timers owe it to themselves to give the tried-and-true itinerary a whirl. First, stop by the tree-shaded central plaza and admire the bandstand and surrounding rose gardens. Next, move on to the Tecate brewery for a tour and tasting at the home of one of Mexico's better beers. Then, treat yourself to one of the delightful restaurants on Callejon Libertad, stopping, before or after your meal, to bargain with the street vendors selling leather goods made from local cattle. The heat, haggling, and good food may exhaust you, but before you leave be sure to stop by El Mejor Pan, Tecate's famous bakery, to pick up a half dozen *churros*, delicious sugar-coated doughnuts. They make the perfect snack for the drive back to San Diego.

PART THREE
◆◆◆◆◆◆◆◆◆◆◆
THE BEST PLACES

Chapter Nine

◆◆◆◆◆◆◆◆◆◆◆

Dining

I T DIDN'T take long for the New World to capture the imagination of the Old. Columbus had no sooner landed on the outlying shores of America than a ragtag armada set forth from Spanish ports, flying "El Dorado or Bust" flags from their masts and carrying adventurers toward the promising new continent.

True, food probably wasn't what the *conquistadors* and clerics were thinking about as they made the difficult passage to America. But conquering and converting were demanding work, and Cortés, Balboa, Coronado, and their men had to eat well. When it came time to eat, the Spaniards who came to the New World were far more receptive to the offerings of pre-Columbian civilization than is commonly thought.

They wasted no time, in fact, seizing upon America's culinary treasury and incorporating it into their diets. A thousand New Worlds could not have slaked the conquerors' thirst for gold and glory, but the Spaniards' appetite for adventure was satisfied by the continent's corn, pota-

toes, cocoa, peanuts, chiles, tomatoes, papayas, and pine-
apples.

For the next two hundred years, the New World and
its exotic promise sustained the hopes, fed the imagination, and filled the bellies of the generations of Spaniards
who were drawn to its shores. But as the newcomers
pushed the boundaries of New Spain further north, into
the beautiful but arid regions of California, the New
World offered diminishing returns. For the Franciscan
friars who moved into Southern California during the
eighteenth century, things got grim fast. Setting up headquarters in present-day San Diego, Father Junípero Serra
and his fellow priests found a few receptive souls but
precious little in the way of decent grub.

By all accounts, San Diego remained a desert for gour-
mands well into the twentieth century. Although American steakhouses, Continental dining rooms, and
neighborhood Mexican restaurants offering honest,
straightforward fare opened up over the years, one still
had to go to Los Angeles or San Francisco for a truly first-
rate dining experience.

Thankfully, all that's changed. In recent years a new
wave of culinary adventurers has run up on San Diego's
shores. They've gone about rescuing the local dining scene
with missionary zeal.

The real sea change occurred during the late 1970s and
early '80s, when San Diego restaurateurs participated in
the creation of "California cuisine." Like France's *nou-
velle cuisine*, the new California cookery emphasized light
sauces, regional ingredients, startling presentations, and
small portions. The development of a local style of cooking was a welcome declaration of culinary independence;
unfortunately, it created a generation of kitchen mini-
malists, who served increasingly skimpy portions at increasingly exorbitant prices.

The good news is that California cuisine's hold on the city has loosened. Today, San Diego has more than a thousand restaurants, providing eaters with plenty of dining alternatives. San Diego's dining scene also has experienced a healthy internationalization, with kabobs, focaccia, and pho now easier to find than a cheeseburger in some parts of town. But don't fear: There are still plenty of eateries in town where you can enjoy entrées as traditional as beef Wellington or as unreconstructed as meatloaf.

Although the restaurants described in this chapter vary in cuisine and ambience, all offer good food and good service at fair prices. Some, like Canes in Hillcrest, are well-known; others are still underappreciated. Except where noted, dress is casual (no jacket required). None of the restaurants included here turn away families, but eateries that are especially child-friendly are so labeled.

The cost of a dinner for two, including tax, tip, and a drink or two, is still quite reasonable in San Diego. Prices for two are rated by the following scale: $25 or less, Cheap; $26 to $40, Inexpensive; $41 to $60, Moderate; $61 to $100, Expensive; and more than $100, Very Expensive. The area code for all phone numbers is 619. Credit cards are: AE, American Express; DIS, Discovery; MC, MasterCard; and V, Visa.

Highly Recommended

ANTHONY'S STAR OF THE SEA ROOM. With meticulously prepared entrées, disciplined service, and an elegant dining room, Anthony's Star of the Sea Room is San Diego's premier seafood house. Every year, the restaurant garners top honors in surveys of local diners, even though some critics insist the cart service is stodgy and dated. Nature lovers may find the early evening views of busy North

Island Naval Air Station a one-star letdown; but once the sun sets, the air base disappears into the night and diners enjoy the dazzling dance of the city's lights on the harbor waters. The kitchen uses the freshest ingredients and puts out unparalleled snapper, salmon, and scampi. When it's in season, the abalone is *the* entrée to try.

1360 N. Harbor Drive at Ash Street, downtown. 232-7408. Open daily for dinner. Reservations necessary. Coat and tie required. Expensive to Very Expensive. AE, DIS, MC, V.

BUSALACCHI'S. Busalacchi's is a delicious reminder that you can enjoy Sicilian fare without running the risk of bruising your head on an overhanging Chianti bottle. Set in what once was a private home, the restaurant successfully updates and interprets the traditional foods of Sicily. The kitchen puts out a remarkably light *spaghetti alla melanzane*, and excels with inventive and flavorful treats like *pasta con sardi*, an aggressive pasta dish that features pine nuts, anchovies, and raisins. On warm nights, the patio in front is especially pleasant.

3681 Fifth Avenue, between Brookes and Pennsylvania, in Hillcrest. Open Monday through Friday for lunch, daily for dinner. Moderate to Expensive. AE, DIS, MC, V.

CANES CALIFORNIA BISTRO. George and Piret Munger, the owners of Canes, are the undisputed First Couple of San Diego cookery. During the 1970s and '80s, they revolutionized the local palate with their collection of Piret's bistros and Perfect Pan shops and cooking schools. Their efforts to demystify and popularize good, honest cooking paid off handsomely in 1985, when ViCorp, a huge food service conglomerate, purchased the couple's bistros, stockpots and all. Today, the Mungers are back, presiding over Canes California Bistro, a cheery, laid-back eatery with contemporary appeal that continues Piret's tradition of unpretentious excellence. Canes offers hearty food at wonderful prices, including *tourte au chou*, a delightful pork and cabbage pie, and lemon-roasted chicken, both popular holdovers from the old days. The pizzas and pastas are exceptional buys and highly recommended. Although the waiters and waitresses are casually dressed, service is professionally brisk and attentive. With its proximity to the theaters of Balboa Park, Canes has become a real favorite with theatergoers and actors and actresses who appreciate George's unassuming manner. The bar is very small but very friendly. Carry-out is available.

1270 Cleveland Avenue, in the Uptown District of Hillcrest. 299-3551. Open daily for lunch and dinner. Reservations suggested. Inexpensive to Moderate. DIS, MC, V.

CASA DE BANDINI. Often overlooked by hungry eaters dashing to the more popular Casa de Pico in the Bazaar Del Mundo, Casa de Bandini is the jewel in San Diego's Mexican-food crown. As do most of the restaurants in Old Town, Casa de Bandini serves heaping portions of dependable treats, including delightfully light enchiladas *suizas* and massive *chimichangas*. The difference here is history. Set in Juan Bandini's erstwhile home, where more than one conspiracy was cooked up during San Diego's colorful Mexican years, this restaurant is famous for its secluded back patio, where mariachis strum as they stroll, evoking a romantic world light years removed from Old Town's present-day bustle. Try the nachos with *chorizo* and you'll understand why locals are more than happy to rub shoulders with tourists at this delightful monument to San Diego's wild years.

Next to Seeley Stables on Calhoun Street, Old Town.

297-8211. Cheap to Inexpensive. AE, DIS, MC, V. Great with children.

CASA MAYA. Unpretentious, inexpensive, and largely unknown outside its neighborhood, Casa Maya serves simple, honest Mexican food. What it lacks in elegance it makes up for in taste. One of the favorites here is steak *picada*, sirloin tips simmered with onions, tomatoes, and peppers, which comes with ample portions of rice, beans, and tortillas. Although salads and sandwiches are offered at this pocket-sized diner, stick with the Mexican side of the menu. Try the enchiladas New Mexico style, three rich cheese enchiladas served on a bed of lettuce and tomatoes and crowned with a fried egg. The restaurant's jukebox, which features artists like Los Invasores, Los Caminantes, and Jesse Salcido, provides wonderful background music. Casa Maya is a terrific place for breakfast, lunch, or dinner.

4201 Park Boulevard, between University and El Cajon Boulevard. 299-5528. Cheap. Cash only. Great with children.

CORVETTE DINER, T-BIRD DINER, AND GALAXY GRILL. These three chrome-plated shrines to America's confident years offer no-frills, stick-to-your-ribs fare. The new T-Bird (601 N. Broadway, Escondido) and Galaxy Grill (on Horton Plaza's Restaurant Row, downtown) continue owner David Cohn's dedication to retro madness and vintage fun, but a trip to the kitschy Corvette is most recommended. The cavernous dining room is a rambunctious tribute to the products and icons of the 1950s and '60s—especially big, beautiful cars—and a revolving collection of mint-condition Corvettes serves as the restaurant's centerpiece. The perky, costumed waitresses sometimes go overboard, but the memorabilia-driven zaniness is infectious. And the food is great. The menu features a zesty Cincinnati three-way chili, meatloaf better than your mom ever made, and daily blue-plate specials. The Corvette's extravagance carries through to the portions, which are, in a word, enormous. The Rory burger, a stock slider souped up with peanut butter and bacon, is an unexpected delight. The no-reservations policy makes long lines likely on most evenings. One-hour waits are not uncommon on weekends.

3946 Fifth Avenue near Washington Street, Hillcrest. 542-1001. Cheap to inexpensive. DIS, MC, V. Fantastic with children.

FONTAINEBLEAU ROOM. This posh eatery on the second floor of the Little America Hotel puts out respectable Continental dishes during the week, but the weekend brunches are especially substantial and satisfying. All the conventional brunch entrées are offered here, including made-to-order omelets, delightful salads, lox and bagels, and, for dessert, excellent cakes and fresh fruit. Service is staid and competent. The Fontainebleau fills up very quickly on the weekends, so reservations here are a must. You can dress up for this one if you like, but it's certainly not required.

1055 Second Avenue, downtown. 238-1818. Moderate to expensive. MC, V.

THE FRENCH SIDE OF THE WEST. Few restaurants in San Diego offer fixed-price limited-choice menus. Fewer still offer the option at a price within reason. A welcome exception to this rule is The French Side of the West, a small, attractive establishment that has transformed San Diego's conception of French cuisine. Like its flagstone floors, the restaurant's simple fare is reminiscent of what you would find in a small French-provincial inn. Although the featured items in the five-course meals vary each night, the kitchen incorporates seasonal items into all its dishes. Given the daily change of menus, it's difficult to recommend particular choices. Still, the *coq au vin*, a hearty rendition of the enduring classic, and the steak with white peppercorn sauce are among the restaurant's strong suits. The best way to prepare for either is with the splendid *salade verte*, tossed to perfection with a sprinkling of *chevre*. Portions are small enough so that all five courses, from appetizer to dessert, can be enjoyed without discomfort. This is a charming and affordable place to dine—if you can squeeze in. Reservations are a must, particularly on weekends. When you call, ask for a table on the patio. Within walking distance of Balboa Park's Simon Edison Centre for the Performing Arts, the French Side of the West offers an early seating for people on their way to an event at the center.

2202 Fourth Avenue near Ivy, downtown. 234-5540. Inexpensive; the fixed-price menu is $16.50. AE, MC, V.

GRANT GRILL. When the historic U.S. Grant Hotel underwent a sorely needed $60-million renovation a few years back, the famous first-floor grill, long a gathering place for the city's political and business elite, was lovingly restored to its turn-of-the-century elegance. Today, this wood-paneled, red-boothed spot is a see-and-be-seen venue for the professional set of both genders, now that the old rule barring women from entering before 5 P.M. has been scrapped. Although the menu has been updated, the famous mock turtle soup is still the restaurant's unbeatable starter; the *crème brulée* remains the dessert to save room for. After dinner you can retire to the adjacent lounge and dance to the standards.

326 Broadway, downtown. 239-6806. Expensive. AE, MC, V.

IL FORNAIO. Il Fornaio has wowed San Diegans with its stunning views of the Pacific, its slick, open-kitchen design, and its fresh ingredients and generous portions. Lunch and dinner are a treat, particularly if you're lucky enough to get a table on the outdoor *piazza*. You might open with the stuffed focaccia and then move on to the angel hair in tomato sauce or one of the many daily specials. The oven turns out crisp pizzas, but the seafood entrées, including squid and shrimp, are superb, making you wonder if a restaurant overlooking the Mediterranean could surpass Il Fornaio.

1555 Camino Del Mar, Del Mar. 755-8876. Inexpensive to moderate. MC, V.

MONTANAS AMERICAN GRILL. This snazzy newcomer has quickly established itself as a heart-of-Uptown favorite, offering regional American cuisine in an ultramodern setting. Not everything is excellent, but the mesquite-grilled entrées stand out, most notably a mixed grill that means business. The bar offers a great selection of handcrafted beers from up and down the West Coast and is a good place to loaf while you wait for your table. In the short time Montanas has been open, it has drawn a number of local luminaries. Their photographs adorn the walls. Its eccentricities—including the bizarre light fixtures—notwithstanding, Montanas offers appetizing upscale fair. The staff is young but alert.

1421 University Avenue. 297-0722. Moderate to expensive.

PHO PASTEUR ANH HONG. Tucked away in a strip mall, this Vietnamese mainstay isn't much to look at, but the food is first-rate. The menu is enormous, the prices are rock bottom, and the service is conscientious and swift. Not surprisingly, pho—a delicately nuanced beef soup with rice noodles and meat toppings—is the item of

choice here, but other Vietnamese favorites, hot pots especially, are quite good. The shrimp and pork rolls, wrapped
in rice paper, are among the restaurant's very best dishes.
Everything here has the hint of mint, cilantro, citrus, and
. . . magic. Although Pho Pasteur offers competently prepared Chinese entrées, it's best to ignore these dishes in
favor of the Vietnamese specialties.

   7612 Linda Vista Road, Linda Vista. 569-7515. Cheap.
MC, V.

ROBERTO'S; RUBIO'S. California has produced more fran-
chised eating establishments than anyone would care to
admit. But when San Diegans are in the mood for a quick
bite, the destination of choice is Roberto's or Rubio's, two
locally owned small chains that put out straightforward
Mexican food in short order. Rubio's has singlehandedly
popularized the fish taco, a lightly fried fish fillet, covered
in a tart white sauce, garnished with cabbage, and served
piping hot in a corn tortilla. Roberto's excels with first-
rate *carne asada* burritos, *tacquitos*, and enchiladas. The
extensive menus at both operations take time to absorb,
but the turnaround time on orders is dizzying. Roberto's
(755-1629) and Rubio's (270-4800) have locations
throughout the county, so call for the one nearest you.
Cheap.

SAMSON'S. With the opening of a second SamSon's in the
area, lovers of hearty and wholesome Jewish cooking now
have a choice of noshing in the original restaurant in La
Jolla or in the attractive new spot at 501 W. Broadway,
downtown. The restaurant's blintzes, knishes, and deli
sandwiches, served in enormous portions, are excellent at
both locations. The breakfasts are especially impressive,
with the reuben omelet taking top honors for imagination
and taste. The delicatessen/bakery at the La Jolla location
offers pickled tongue, kishke, smoked fish, corned beef,

and pastrami as well as wonderful challa, streudel, ku-
chen, and hamantaschen.

8861 Villa La Jolla Drive near La Jolla Village Drive,
La Jolla. 455-1461. DIS, MC, V.

SAMMY'S WOODFIRED PIZZA. Tabs are low at this good-
natured Neapolitan restaurant in the heart of La Jolla that
creates over twenty gourmet pizzas in a traditional wood-
burning stove. The California twist comes from the toppings, which range from the straightforward (tomato and
cheese) to the truly twisted (Peking duck?). The pastas
and salads are good standbys, but the signature dishes are
the pizzas. Sammy's has wine and beer at attractive prices,
and the place is fun for the kids.

702 Pearl Street, La Jolla. 456-5222. Cheap to inexpensive. MC, V.

SHEIK RESTAURANT. The appetizers, or *mazzas*, are so
good at this tapestry-lined Lebanese hole-in-the-wall that
you could forgo the entrées entirely and create a meal
from the delightful hors d'oeuvres here, including hum-
mus, tabouli, kafta, and pickled turnips. But given the
remarkable quality of the main courses, consider saving
room. The best dishes are rolled grape leaves, rotisserie
lemon chicken, shish kebab, and the distinctively seasoned
pilafs. The wailing background music shouldn't unnerve
you: Simon, the Sheik's unflappable host, is extremely
friendly and largely responsible for building the loyal following the restaurant enjoys. Eating with your fingers is
very big here, so the kids will love it.

2664 Fifth Avenue, downtown/Hillcrest. 234-5888.
Closed Sunday and Monday. Moderate. AE, MC, V.

WATERFRONT BAR & GRILL. Legend has it this was the
first San Diego bar to reopen after Prohibition was lifted
in 1933. Today the Waterfront is home to one of the best

à la carte brunches in town, especially if you like Mexican food. The grub, it's true, won't win the bar any Michelin stars, but the Waterfront's simple preparations and rock-bottom prices have turned this former fisherman's haunt into a must-do weekend-morning destination for adventuresome diners. The best items are from the Mexican side of the menu, although the *carnitas* are not recommended. Try the *machaca* platter, a heaping plate of eggs scrambled with green peppers, tomatoes, onions, cheese, and shredded beef, served with steaming flour tortillas, rice, and beans. The Bloody Marys are zesty and make a good starter. The airy, relaxed atmosphere makes this funky spot a perfect place to pass a relaxing afternoon. Because the Waterfront is really a bar, folks under 21 are prohibited from entering by state law.

2044 Kettner Boulevard, near downtown. 232-9656. Cheap. Cash only.

YOSHINO. This bustling Japanese restaurant is noteworthy not only for its fine, reasonably priced food but for its endearing floor staff as well. The kimonoed waitresses here come across as somewhat giddy, but they deliver the restaurant's entrées with astonishing speed and accuracy. Yoshino's word-of-mouth reputation for excellence created long lines a few year back, forcing the owners to abandon their original digs and move next door. Though simply appointed, the new restaurant serves up the same superb standard treats, including excellent beef and chicken teriyaki and a fabulous *katzu don*. The chief reason to visit Yoshino's is the sashimi, which is simply the freshest in the country. You can get a huge portion of this impossibly pink, mouth-watering delicacy by ordering the Yoshino Special, a fixed-price, four-course feast, which also includes a delicate shrimp-and-vegetable tempura, sesame chicken, and an unparalleled sukiyaki loaded with spinach, tofu, onions, glass noodles, and paper-thin slices of what you will swear is Kobi beef.

1790 W. Washington Street at India Street, Mission Hills. 295-2232. Closed Mondays. Moderate. AE, MC, V.

Recommended Downtown

Several very good restaurants in the downtown area offer inexpensive ethnic food. For Mexican food, try Alfonso's, 135 Broadway (234-7300), next to the Spreckels Theater. Like its counterpart in La Jolla, the downtown Alfonso's features tasty south-of-the-border standards, including a simple but toothsome *carne asada* burrito.

San Diego's oldest Chinese restaurant, Wong's Nanking Cafe, 467 Fifth Avenue (239-2171), is worth a visit. Although their legacy is less apparent outside San Francisco, the Chinese played a central role in the development of California during the late nineteenth and early twentieth centuries. Wong's is one of the few remaining vestiges of that heritage in San Diego—a town that shamelessly permitted its once-bustling Chinatown to be demolished in the name of "development." Although Wong's has only been here since 1940, Chinese food has been served on the premises since 1920. The Cantonese entrées are good but not great; the atmosphere and streamlined deco decor are tops.

Mary Pappas's Athens Market Taverna, 109 F Street (234-1955), has been hailed as one of the best Greek restaurants in town for over a decade now. The Greek-style chicken, delicately spiced with oregano, is a favorite, but the lamb and pork sausages with orange peel are wonderful too.

If you're in a Mediterranean mood but would prefer a snazzier setting, there's Sfuzzi at 340 Fifth Avenue (231-2323). Unfortunately, you'll probably have to wait, because this recent arrival has quickly established a reputation for very good Italian food. The *pizzetas*, or stuffed pizzas, are quite good, delicate but certainly not bland. The spinach lasagna, prepared with grilled chicken and sautéed mushrooms, the fettucine *pomodoro*, and the veal scaloppine with wild mushrooms are also fine choices. Sfuzzi is part of a small chain, with spots in New York, Washington, D.C., Houston, and Denver, but the food has a not-to-be-missed local flavor.

Tambo de Oro, at 530 B Street (231-0801), provides another perspective on downtown. Formerly a private club, the restaurant perched on the eleventh floor of the Union Bank building, now opens its doors to the public for lunch and dinner. The menu is competently Continental but the real star here is the sweeping view of downtown.

In another league is Mister A's, atop the Fifth Avenue Financial Center at 2550 Fifth Avenue (239-1377). This heavy, masculine hideaway has unsurpassed views of downtown, Balboa Park, the harbor, and beyond. Mister A's serves traditional Continental favorites, including rack of lamb and beef Wellington, in its red-velveted dining room. Good food and good views do indeed go together at Mister A's. Reservations are necessary and coats and ties are required at this very pricey San Diego institution.

Sanfilippo, at 3515 Fifth Avenue (299-6080), is a down-to-earth Italian alternative, dependable for eggplant parmigiana and pizza. The back patio is especially inviting on balmy nights and the rock-bottom prices are always welcome. Sanfilippo is popular with neighborhood residents, who appreciate the unpretentious but reliable food and service. The restaurant is closed Sunday. A block up from Sanfilippo is Stefano's, at 3671 Fifth Avenue (296-0975), one of San Diego's premier Italian restaurants. The crowd that packs in here enjoys exquisitely prepared Northern Italian–style dishes, including a *bistecca alla Florentina* that is unparalleled. Prices are moderate; reservations are advised.

Kung Food, at 2929 Fifth Avenue (298-7302), is one of San Diego's more popular vegetarian retreats. The restaurant offers indoor and outdoor seating, and it does amazing things with bean sprouts and rennetless cheeses. Jimbo's Pizza Naturally, at 3918 30th Street, North Park (294-9611), is an excellent place to go for vegetarian pizzas.

Recommended in La Jolla and North County

As you would expect, there are a number of first-rate restaurants in exclusive La Jolla. The best combine mouth-watering entrées with eye-catching views of the stunning coastline. Elario's, atop the Summer House Inn at 7955 La Jolla Shores Drive (459-0541), and Top o' the Cove, set in a converted bungalow at 1216 Prospect Street (454-7779), are intimate, romantic spots where extravagance is never out of style. Elario's wine list is one of the best in the world, according to *Wine Spectator*, and Top o' the Cove has more than nine hundred selections in its own award-winning cellar. Panoramic views make both restaurants agreeable spots, though your accountant may beg to differ: These are very expensive eateries indeed. Jackets are suggested at both restaurants, and reservations are required.

La Valencia's Sky Room, at 1132 Prospect Street, has great views of the La Jolla shoreline and a $38 *prix fixe* menu (wine and dessert extra). Make reservations: The tenth-floor Sky Room has only 12 tables, each with a stunning view, and so the room tends to sell out quickly. Another reliable spot in La Jolla, though removed from the village, is Cindy Black's at 5721 La Jolla Boulevard (456-6299), where Black, an award-winning chef, interprets the classic dishes of France with innovation and panache.

If you're looking for more moderate prices, check out Jose's Courtroom, 1037 Prospect Street (454-7655), or the Hard Rock Cafe, 909 Prospect Street (454-5101). Both offer consistently good food in rollicking settings. Jose's serves Mexican food at a good price and the restaurant's island bar is a great spot to sit and gawk at the well-dressed strollers who pass by on their way to some of the more expensive bistros on Prospect.

Further north, Cilantros, at 3702 Via de la Valle, Del Mar (259-8777), is a good dinner choice, particularly if Southwestern cuisine is your thing. Patio dining is available but the indoor dining is a touch more graceful. Closer to Del Mar Racetrack is Taryn's at the Track, 514 Via de la Valle (481-8300). Pizzas, seafood, and pasta are safe bets here. The Fish Market, 640 Via de la Valle (755-2277), is another odds-on favorite with visiting bettors and area diners, paying off with very fresh seafood and reasonable prices. Scalini, further up the valley at 3790 Via de la Valle (259-9994), offers moderately priced California cuisine and an exceptional view of the neighboring Rancho Santa Fe Polo Club.

Recommended Elsewhere

CORONADO. The current favorite is Azzura Point, at Loews Coronado Bay Resort, 4000 Coronado Bay Road (424-4000), which serves seafood with Asian influences. Mexican Village, at 120 Orange Avenue (435-1822), is still popular, with dependable Mexican treats (including a unique potato taco) and, curiously enough, the best fish and chips in town. Every Sunday, the Hotel del Coronado, 1500 Orange Avenue (435-6611), has locals mingling with visitors beneath chandeliers and a sugar-pine ceiling when it puts out a sumptuous brunch in the magnificent Crown Room.

DESERTS AND MOUNTAINS. In the desert community of Borrego Springs, the pickings are slim. The dining rooms at La Casa del Zorro (767-5323) and neighboring Ram's Hill (767-5000) serve well-prepared high-end fare, but they may be too dressy if you're coming off a daylong hike in the dusty desert. If you are, do not fear: There are a number of casual spots on Palm Canyon Drive worth ducking into, including Little Italy (767-3938), and Las Palmas Bar and Grill, inside the Palm Canyon Resort (767-5341). Both offer well-portioned meals, very reasonable prices, and no dress code. From your table at the Whifferdill restaurant (767-4646), adjacent to the Borrego Springs airport, you can watch student pilots practicing touch-and-go landings.

On Mount Laguna, the only spot open seven days a week is the Sunrise Cafe (473-8415), on Sunrise Highway. The cafe serves breakfast, lunch, and dinner in its pine-log dining room.

MEXICO. As befits a city its size, Tijuana has a vibrant and varied restaurant scene, offering diners everything from dim sum to pizza. Some venues—like Rivoli, in the Hotel Lucerna on Paseo de los Heroes—serve exquisite Continental dishes in plush surroundings. But first-time visitors are best advised to sample Tijuana's many reasonably priced Mexican and Spanish restaurants, whose friendly English-speaking waiters serve entrées that bear surprisingly little resemblance to what's called Mexican fare north of the border.

La Costa, on Calle 7 between Revolución and Constitución (858494), offers delightfully prepared Mexican seafood specialties, decent prices, and a relaxed, family setting. The *sopa de siete mares* (Span., seven seas soup) featured here is especially good. Tia Juana Tilly's, at 701 Avenida Revolución (857833), has been a visitor favorite for years. The long lines outside the door attest to the popularity of the restaurant's moderately priced Mexican treats, which include a unique taco platter, large enough for two. Chiki Jai, 1050 Avenida Revolución (854955), offers inexpensive entrées from Spain's Basque region, and a delightful paella on Sundays. But it can't compare with La Taberna Española, 1001 Paseo de los Heroes (847562), which tempts with an extensive *tapas* menu, sawdust-covered floors, a cozy setting, and moderate prices. Bol Corona, 520 Avenida Revolución (857940), specializes in piquant Mexican soups and toothsome burritos and is open from 7 A.M. to 4 A.M. every day of the week. Cafe La Especial, just south of Bol Corona and down a flight of stairs, is a friendly, easygoing spot with conventional Mexican entrées, delightful desserts, and rock-bottom tabs.

If you're heading down the Baja peninsula toward Rosarito or Ensenada, be sure to stop by Puerto Nuevo, a former fishing village about thirty-five miles south of Tijuana on the coastal toll road (at kilometer marker 44). Puerto Nuevo is famous for its lobster feasts. There are upwards of twenty small eateries on the town's dusty restaurant row. The current favorite seems to be Restaurant Puerto Nuevo No. 1. Look for the little yellow house and the long lines of tourists licking their chops. Prices at most of the restaurants here run in the $10 range for a small lobster and in the $20 range for a large one, served, of course, Puerto Nuevo–style, with plenty of refried beans, fresh tortillas, rice, salsa, and limes.

MISSION BEACH AND PACIFIC BEACH. The wood-paneled dining room at Saska's, 3768 Mission Boulevard (488-

7311), is somewhat dated, but this steak-and-seafood house is still one of the best spots on the beach; it's especially good for a late-night meal. Giulio's, at 809 Thomas Avenue in Pacific Beach (483-7726), offers memorable Italian dishes with moderate to expensive tabs.

Chapter Ten
♦♦♦♦♦♦♦♦♦♦♦

Lodging

WITH forty-five thousand hotel rooms, San Diego offers a host of accommodation options for the leisure or business traveler. All those choices can make decision-making difficult, however, so here's some help.

First a word on location: If you're planning to visit Balboa Park, Horton Plaza, the Gaslamp Quarter, the Convention Center, or any of the city's beaches, most of the hotels in downtown, Hotel Circle, or the beach cities will provide quick and convenient access. And, even though they're removed from many of the city's bigger attractions, like Sea World and the San Diego Zoo, the inns and resorts of the mountain and desert areas of the county are worth considering as well, especially if you're also planning a trip into the county's breathtaking back country.

The hotels and inns described here offer local color and local character and are within easy reach of most of the landmarks, museums, and other attractions covered in this book. They're listed below by location and by price. All rates are subject to the city's 9 percent transient-occupancy tax.

If you plan to be in San Diego for a week or more, and if you want to stay near the water, consider the option of a short- or long-term beach rental. A number of firms lease condos and apartments in Mission Beach and Pacific Beach, including Beach and Bayside Vacations (488-3691), Beach Connection (456-9411), Penny Realty (539-3910), San Diego Vacation Rentals (296-1000), and the Mission Beach Management Company (488-3100). During the peak season, from mid-June to mid-August, Beach and Bayside Vacations rents a fully-equipped two-bedroom condo on the beach or bay in South Mission Beach for about $1,500 a week; condos and homes just a few steps back from the water can be had for around $1,000. Although advance planning is recommended (forty percent of the short-term summer rentals are booked by mid-January), last-minute cancellations often free up units for temporizing travelers. During the off-season, rates for these rentals drop by as much as one-half, and September—when school is back in session and families are out of the vacation-rental market—seems to be the cheapest month of all.

During the summer months, many college students who live in the beach area abandon their school-year digs to go back home, and property management companies try to fill the temporary vacancies by renting these units to unsuspecting vacationers. The best advice is to avoid these "bargains." They're cheaper, it's true, but they tend to have few amenities—except for leftover beer kegs and stained carpets. The best vacation-rental accommodations are properties devoted to that purpose year-round. They're professionally decorated, well-maintained, and equipped with everything from espresso machines to VCRs to washers and dryers. They permit you to get a real feel for the community without slumming it.

If you're going to be in town for an extended period of time, consider a longer-term beach rental. You'll not only enjoy a 10 to 15 percent discount on the standard rate, but you'll also avoid paying the city's 9 percent transient-occupancy tax, which hotels and motels are required to collect.

Recommended Luxury Hotels and Resorts
The Beaches

CATAMARAN RESORT HOTEL. When the Evans family, owners of the Catamaran and her cross-bay sister hotel, the Bahia, decided to renovate the aging "Cat" back in 1987, they meant business. Not content with a mere makeover of the aging grande dame of Pacific Beach, they rolled up their sleeves and gave her a complete facelift. They added five new delightfully designed wings, a spectacular new lobby (complete with waterfall and squawking macaws), a new restaurant and bar, and a swimming pool, Jacuzzi, and exercise room. The hotel's Polynesian theme—somewhat incongruous in Spanish-settled San Diego—remains, with plenty of rattan furniture in the 315 guest rooms and lots of lush ferns throughout the upgraded grounds.

As a result, the Catamaran once again is worthy of its location. Just a block away from the ocean, the hotel's quiet, secluded bayside setting seems a million miles away from the boardwalk bustle. Sailboats, sailboards, pedalboats, and, naturally, catamarans are available for an extra charge to guests who want to play on the bay. Rates here range from $120 for a standard room to $225 for one of the hotel's spacious suites. The Cannibal Bar, the hotel's noisy tavern, features live entertainment.

The Catamaran is not without its drawbacks. Although the family-owned operation prides itself on friendliness and personal service, those members of the staff who aren't Evanses may strike some observers as excessively laid-back. The hotel also charges guests $4 a night for parking in the adjacent parking structure, a rather petty dig considering the price of rooms here. But the tasteful renovation, perfect setting, and other amenities make up for the few flaws, and the Catamaran is a good option for visitors who refuse to compromise on location.

3999 Mission Boulevard, Pacific Beach; 619-488-1081.

COLONIAL INN. This cozy neo-Colonial hostelry has been an integral part of La Jolla's downtown cityscape since 1913, when it welcomed its first guest. A wholesale restoration and redecoration project, completed in the summer of 1991, brightened up this handsome landmark, keeping the old-fashioned charm and warmth intact while enhancing the inn's modern conveniences. The attractive lobby has hints of Art Deco; the inner courtyard beyond, which houses the hotel's pool and pleasant garden, is a lush hideaway from the commercial commotion on Prospect Street.

The 67 rooms and seven suites here were tastefully redone during the recent refurbishment, with peach and taupe hues dominating. The rates range from $150 per night to $250, single or double occupancy. The oceanside rooms and suites are at the upper end of the range, but the less-expensive rooms, which overlook Prospect Street, are just as nice. Nonsmoking rooms are available. The rate includes complimentary Continental breakfast and front-door valet service—no small consideration in La Jolla, where parking can be frustrating. The turn-down service, complimentary mineral water, and free morning newspaper are also nice touches.

Putnam's, the restaurant at the Colonial Inn, is pretty good for a hotel bistro, and Chef Smedley serves attractive breakfasts, lunches, dinners, and weekend brunches. High tea—featuring scones, Devonshire cream, and plenty of hot tea—is celebrated Wednesday through Sunday, from 3 P.M. to 5 P.M.

910 Prospect Street, La Jolla; 619-454-2181.

CORONADO VICTORIAN HOUSE. Bonnie Marie Kinosian, the long-time dance instructor who owns this charming three-story inn, performed a difficult tango getting the city of Coronado to license her circa-1894 house as a bed-and-breakfast. To begin with, opposition from city residents was fierce. Eventually Kinosian and her Coronado neighbors reached a compromise. The city issued a special variance, which permitted Kinosian to run this blue, gray, and burgundy house as a bed-and-breakfast inn—but only on weekends and religious holidays and then only if the guests also enrolled in one of Kinosian's dance classes. Try writing a marketing brochure that explains *that* to a potential guest.

Eventually, however, Kinosian was able to dance around that spot of trouble, and today visitors can stay at the Coronado Victorian House seven nights a week. Lodgers no longer are required to dance before dozing, either, although Kinosian is more than willing to sweep guests into her adjoining dance studio and teach them ballroom, tap, or belly-dancing. The guest rooms, each named after a famous dancer or artist ("The Baryshnikov," "The Fred & Ginger"), are equipped with antique brass and sleigh beds, 100-year-old Persian rugs, old-fashioned claw-foot bathtubs, and a variety of other period pieces. Guests are given a key to the front door upon arrival and are invited to treat the inn, which is situated in a lovely residential neighborhood, as their home away from home. The meals, which often feature items like homemade yogurt and a sinful baklava that bespeak Kinosian's Lebanese heritage, are served on flatware from the eighteenth century. Guests may eat in the dining room or out on the patio. If you like a particular dish, Kinosian is more than happy to provide you with the recipe. Though pricey, this is an eccentric, happy place.

Rates here range from $199 to $599 a day, depending on how many meals and how many dance lessons guests take.

1000 Eighth Street, Coronado; phone 619-435-2200.

HOTEL DEL CORONADO. This Queen Anne–style seaside resort, with its red-shingled cupolas and grand entryway, is one of San Diego's most recognized landmarks and easily its most famous inn. Some might argue that superlatives were invented to help visitors describe this grand old hotel. It is, to begin with, the largest beachfront hotel on the North American Pacific Coast, with 700 rooms sprawled out over 34 acres of prime waterfront property. It's also one of the oldest hostelries in the country. Built in 1888, the Del is filled with a sense of history—not at all faded, thanks to conscientious upkeep by the hotel's owner, Larry Lawrence. There are the physical reminders of the past, of course, including three bird-cage elevators, reportedly the oldest operating lifts of their kind in the world. There are the memories as well, of visits by 12 U.S. presidents, dozens of foreign dignitaries and royals, and hundreds of celebrities, including Ramon Navarro, Jack Dempsey, Babe Ruth, Marilyn Monroe, Tony Curtis, and Mary Martin.

The lobby and mezzanine are extraordinarily warm and inviting, with handcrafted mahogany walls and ceilings, a spectacular crystal chandelier, potted palms, and overstuffed chairs. The two main dining rooms, the Crown Room and the dinner-only Prince of Wales, are decorated in the same dark hues, but the Palm Court and the delightful Promenade Deck introduce the light, airy side of the Del—the atmosphere that permeates most of the guest rooms here.

Amenities at the Hotel del Coronado include six lighted

tennis courts, two heated pools, a number of interesting specialty shops, and acres and acres of beach frontage. The hotel has a full-time 25-member activity staff, which plans activities and recreational outings for registered guests. You can arrange a boat charter at the front desk; during the most recent America's Cup races, *Stars and Stripes*, the 65-foot catamaran Dennis Connor sailed to victory during the 1988 America's Cup Challenge, was available.

The Del's activity staff runs many events geared to children, providing harried parents with an opportunity to rekindle the romance. And, let's face it: If you can't jump-start your love life here, it's in *serious* trouble. Where else can you dine and dance to the strains of big band or share a bottle of bubbly as Johnny "Ace" Harris, one of the original Ink Spots, croons his way through "I Don't Want to Set The World On Fire"?

Rooms in the original five-story main building run from $149 a night to $199; the rooms overlooking the ocean are at the higher end of the range. Inexplicably, rooms in the newer and, to some minds, less desirable complex, are more expensive—between $189 and $295 per night, with suites in the $450 range. In the estimation of many, the best rooms at the Del are those in the original building with balconies overlooking the delightful inner courtyard, where dozens of local couples exchange wedding vows each year. Suites in this Victorian section are in the $400 range.

1500 Orange Avenue, Coronado; phone 619-522-8000.

LA JOLLA BEACH AND TENNIS CLUB. This ten-acre resort, which has been run by the Kellogg family since it opened in the mid-1920s, is unique in a number of ways, not the least of which is its enviable setting. Nestled on the palm-studded grounds of an exclusive country club, the 91 Spanish-style guest apartments here overlook the club's private beach, located just south of La Jolla Shores.

Summer rates for oceanfront rooms range from $130, for a simple ground-floor unit, to $215, for a second-story suite with three bedrooms, living room, and fully-equipped kitchen. Off-season rates (October through May) are $30 cheaper.

The club's dining room is open for breakfast and lunch, and offers dining alongside the pool. Guests looking for dinner can either step next door, to the Marine Room, or trek a little farther into downtown La Jolla, where a number of wonderful restaurants tempt.

On-site amenities at the La Jolla Beach and Tennis Club are first-class. They include 14 tennis courts (four lighted for night play), a croquet court, an Olympic-size swimming pool, a nine-hole pitch-and-putt golf course, a pro shop, and golf and tennis instruction. A masseuse and a resident hair stylist are on staff as well. Registered guests enjoy the same privileges and white-glove service as regular members, although a small fee is tacked on for golf. The staff is more than willing to help guests arrange deep-sea fishing trips or excursions to nearby championship golf courses.

2000 Spindrift Drive, La Jolla; phone 619-454-7126.

LA COSTA RESORT AND SPA. This full-service resort, situated about thirty-five miles north of downtown San Diego, is not your run-of-the-mill fat farm. It is, to begin with, a member of The Leading Hotels of the World, an exclusive, by-invitation-only association of first-class hostelries. Then there are the people who come here. According to Sports Shinto, the Japanese group that now runs this 400-acre mecca, the average guest at La Costa spends $500 a day while staying here—and that doesn't even include the price of the room. What guests get for their money is access to one of the finest health-and-recreation facilities in the country, with two 18-hole championship golf courses (the PGA pros participate in the Infiniti Tournament of Champions here each year), 23 tennis courts (two grass, four clay, and 17 hard-surface; eight are lighted for night play), separate gyms for men and women, and the world-famous spa facilities of La Costa.

The 474-room complex, which dates from the 1960s, underwent a $100-million renovation and expansion a few years back, and although some might take issue with some of the aesthetic aspects of the overhaul, the result is a thoroughly modern, impeccably operated resort. Because many guests spend their entire vacation on the property, La Costa has the feel of a small city. That sense of place is helped by the presence of six restaurants (including Pisces, an award-winning seafood house, and the Spa Dining Room, which caters to the healthy set with low-calorie, low-fat meals), a 180-seat movie theater, and a small shopping center on the premises. Add to this a first-rate staff that treats every guest like a permanent resident and you begin to understand why visitors return to La Costa year in and year out.

Rates here range from $200 to $300 per night for a standard room, double occupancy. The hotel also offers golf, tennis, and spa packages for those so inclined. The golf package, which includes unlimited green fees, the use of a golf cart, and spa admission, goes for about $300 per couple per night. When you book your room, specify where you want to stay. Guests staying in the 395 standard rooms are placed near the golf course, tennis courts, or spa—according to their preference. The hotel also has 75 one- and two-bedroom suites and four executive houses. Suites start at $375 and go all the way up to $2,000 per night for the Presidential Suite. The two-, four-, and five-bedroom executive homes range from $1,000 to $1,500 per night.

Costa Del Mar Road, Carlsbad; phone 619-438-9111.

La Valencia. Though La Valencia is a decade or so younger than its neighbor, the Colonial Inn, it is perhaps better-known. Originally built as an apartment house, this striking pink stucco building, with its red tile roof, marvelous patios, and sweeping ocean views, was converted into a hotel in the late 1920s, just in time to capitalize on the growing wanderlust of Hollywood types. During the film colony's heyday, Charlie Chaplin, Groucho Marx, and dozens of other celebrities motored down to La Valencia on weekends, where they relaxed and read their scripts in preparation for the following week's shooting. During the 1940s and '50s, the number of celebrity visitors actually increased, as the La Jolla Playhouse brought hundreds of actors and actresses into town during its summer season.

Today, La Valencia is one of the city's finest small inns. Its 105 rooms, each uniquely but tastefully decorated with European flair, add to the hotel's peculiar charm, as does the antique elevator (still staffed by human operator) and the odd floor designations. (For the record, the street-level lobby is actually the seventh floor, with the sixth, fifth, and, finally, fourth floors below, and the eighth, ninth, and tenth above. Plans for the third, second, and first floors—which would have descended toward La Jolla Cove—were dashed by the Depression. Subsequent attempts to renumber the floors were shelved after long-time fans of the hotel protested.) The Whaling Bar, adorned with harpoons, nautical murals, and assorted sailing paraphernalia, is a chatty spot where guests rub shoulders with La Jolla locals. The streetside patio, with its umbrella-covered tables and garden feel, is another delightful spot to unwind, especially on balmy afternoons.

The hotel has a trio of respectable restaurants, but the tenth-floor Sky Room—with just 12 tables overlooking the Cove—is easily the most special, offering à la carte lunches and a recommended fixed-price dinner. But remember to reserve ahead.

Rates range from $135 to $160 for a standard room with a village view; ocean views will run between $170 and $280. Suites at La Valencia fetch from $300 to $600 per night, double occupancy, again depending on the view. The Presidential Suite, a luxurious 800-square-foot penthouse with living room, full entertainment center, Jacuzzi, and stunning ocean view, is $800 per night.

1132 Prospect Street, La Jolla; phone 619-454-0771.

LE MERIDIEN SAN DIEGO. Located in Coronado, just north of the San Diego–Coronado Bay Bridge, Le Meridien is a relative newcomer to the area's lodging scene, with some three hundred rooms—including seven executive suites and a 28-unit villa complex—spread out over its 16 acres. Unobstructed views of the San Diego skyline, coupled with the hotel's good looks, make it a stylish spot to stay in San Diego. Dedicated oceangoers may find its location on San Diego Bay disappointing, but the ocean isn't far away: The public beach outside the Hotel del Coronado is just five minutes away by car. As long as guests remain on the property, however, they have access to Le Meridien's own considerable recreational facilities. These include a full-service spa, offering hydrotherapy baths, herbal wraps, and massages; a health club equipped with Polaris fitness machines, Lifecycles, and Stairmasters; six lighted tennis courts; three pools, including a 75-foot lap pool; and an 18-hole golf course, adjacent to the hotel complex.

Guests at Le Meridien are greeted by the hotel's lobby staff, who are dressed in nautical duds designed by Nina Ricci herself. The sailing motif continues in the rooms themselves, which are supertanker size—standard rooms measure 500 square feet. Suites and villas are larger still. All rooms here come with nice extras, including twice-daily maid service, mini-bars, remote-control televisions, large vanity areas, triple-sheeted beds, three telephones, hair dryers, extra-thick towels, and plush terry robes. The studio and one- and two-bedroom suites in the villa complex surround a pool and whirlpool, but the majority of these deluxe accommodations have in-room Jacuzzis as well.

Le Meridien is affiliated with Air France, and the hotel's Gallic connection carries through to its interior design, which evokes the feeling of a French country villa—albeit a French country villa on the edge of a California bay. Francophiles should note that the hotel hosts an annual Beaujolais Nouveau festival in November, toasting the arrival of the new wine and celebrating the chain's French-inspired flavor.

Rates here range from $165 to $255 for standard rooms and from $205 to $650 for the villas, double occupancy. The hotel also offers spa packages, which range in price from $320 for a two-day package to $865 for a four-day stay; the spa rates are per person, double occupancy.

2000 Second Street, Coronado; phone 619-435-3000.

LOEWS CORONADO BAY RESORT. Opened in the fall of 1991, this $80-million, 14-acre bayside resort boasts 440 rooms and 37 suites. Practically everything is ideal at Loews except its location. On the eastern side of the Silver Strand, three miles south of Coronado, the hotel is some-what removed from the city's life. Views from the hotel's private peninsula are unspectacular by local standards as well—a fact, however, which is frankly reflected in the room rates: Loews is perhaps the only hostelry in Califor-nia where rooms overlooking the pool are actually more expensive than those with a water view. The rates range from $150 to $195 for a standard room and from $225 to $1,100 for a suite.

The amenities at Loews are superb. All guests enjoy nighttime turn-down service, and every room has a built-in entertainment center, two telephones, a fully-equipped balcony, and an ultramodern bath with a Japanese-style soaking tub. Boaters will be most impressed with Loews. The hotel's 80-slip private marina, with its large turning basin, is capable of handling 140-foot so-called "mega-yachts." Sailboats are available for an extra charge to guests who didn't arrive onboard their own. Beach access is via a private pedestrian walkway, which travels underneath the busy highway that cuts off the hotel from the oceanfront.

The restaurants at Loews are Azzura Point, which features innovative seafood entrées with Asian influences, and RRR's Cafe. (The latter is named for the nautical mnemonic "Red, Right, Returning.") Both are quite good. There are five tennis courts, two Jacuzzis, and a well-equipped fitness center with a steam room. A convenient water taxi service is available to whisk guests away to downtown Coronado or across the Bay to San Diego.

4000 Coronado Bay Road, Coronado; phone 619-424-4000.

Downtown

MARRIOTT HOTEL AND MARINA. This handsome hotel and meeting complex is located on the harbor between the San Diego Convention Center and Seaport Village. The two reflecting towers, designed to look like sails filled with wind, have small but attractively decorated rooms with good views of the city and harbor. The marina, pool, restaurants, and lobby are all first-rate, and the staff is congenial. The hotel is geared toward conventioneers and business visitors; pleasure travelers looking to immerse themselves in the city may feel isolated from local life. But the nearby San Diego Trolley stop does provide quick access into the city. Rooms range from $150 to $200 per night. Suites start at $350.

333 West Harbor Drive, downtown; phone 619-234-1500.

WESTGATE HOTEL. A luxurious landmark, within easy walking distance of Horton Plaza, the Gaslamp Quarter, Copley Symphony Hall, and the Bay, the Westgate has 223 rooms and 11 suites, all exquisitely furnished in traditional styles. Amenities are, for the most part, quite modern, and include two-line speaker phones (with computer hookup), remote-control television, and honor bars. Guests have access to the hotel's stunning third-floor outdoor terrace and a free limousine service stands ready to shuttle shoppers and sightseers to downtown attractions. There is, unfortunately, no pool on the premises, but the attentive service and prime location make this one of downtown's most attractive temporary addresses. The Westgate is the only hotel in the city that can claim membership in The Leading Hotels of the World—the same exclusive, by-invitation-only association to which Carlsbad's La Costa Resort and Spa belongs.

Rates range from $144 to $164 for a standard room, double occupancy; special weekend rates drop as low as $110. Suites start at $375.

1055 Second Avenue, downtown; phone 619-238-1818.

The Mountains and Desert

JULIAN HOTEL. One of the county's oldest and loveliest bed-and-breakfast inns, the Julian Hotel is located about sixty miles northeast of downtown San Diego in the mountain town of Julian, where an autumn apple festival and—believe it or not—a summer weed show draw large numbers of tourists. The hotel, listed on the National Register of Historic Places, was originally built in 1897 by Albert and Margaret Robinson, two of San Diego County's first black residents, who earlier had established a reputation for hospitality and warmth with a bakery and restaurant they'd operated during Julian's gold-mining years.

Today, Steve and Gig Ballinger own the Julian Hotel. They've furnished its 18 guest rooms with period antiques and old-fashioned charm. Some of the nicest touches come from the Ballinger's refusal to surrender to modernity. If you stay here, be prepared to do without a television or a phone, because Gig and Steve—bless their hearts—don't see any reason why you should be bothered while you're in Julian. The detached Honeymoon House, with its romantic fireplace, is the largest of the Julian Hotel's accommodations, but the quaint patio cottages are comfortable nesting spots for cooing couples as well. The complimentary breakfasts are huge, featuring goodies like eggs Florentine, fresh fruit, juice, and coffee—and, if you're lucky, some toasted raisin-nut bread from Dudley's Bakery in nearby Santa Ysabel.

Weekday rates at this historic charmer range from $64 for a double or twin with a shared bath to $110 for the Honeymoon House. Weekend rates range from $82 to $145. If you're traveling alone, the Ballingers offer an unbeatable bargain—a $38 rate, good weekdays and weekends, on the double or twin room with shared bath. 2032 Main Street, Julian; phone 619-765-0201. The address for written enquiries is P.O. Box 1856, Julian, CA 92036.

LA CASA DEL ZORRO. La Casa del Zorro (Span., house of the fox) is a 34-acre hideaway resort in the desert town of Borrego Springs, two hours northeast by car from downtown San Diego. It's an elegant spot to pitch your base camp as you explore the surrounding 600,000-acre Anza-Borrego Desert State Park.

Originally built during the 1940s, La Casa del Zorro emerged in the late 1960s as an alternative to the often overcrowded resorts of Palm Springs; yet it remains one of the San Diego area's best-kept hotel secrets. The 77-room complex offers suites and one-, two-, and three-bedroom *casitas* tastefully decorated in subdued Southwestern motifs, with exposed wooden beams and striking whitewashed walls.

Although four of the larger suites here have private pools, there are seven Jacuzzis and three heated pools open to all registered guests. Rooms and suites without desert views overlook these pools. There are six tennis courts (all are lighted for night play, an important consideration in the hot summer months), a pro shop, and a putting green for golfers who want to perfect their putt before moving on to the course at neighboring Ram's Hill. Tandem bicycles, massage therapy, VCRs and movies, and desert guides are available for an extra charge.

The hotel's main dining room, the Butterfield Room, serves American and Continental dishes with some Mexican specialties.

In-room and poolside dining are available.

La Casa del Zorro's rates are from $98 to $450 per night, double occupancy. The rates drop during the summer, when the temperatures soar. A deluxe suite that fetches $300 during the peak season drops to $155 during the hottest part of summer, and the four-bedroom *casita*, which normally goes for $450, falls to $200 on weekdays and $250 on weekends. The resort also offers special weekend tennis clinics with resident pro Gary Lindstrom. Call for information.

3845 Yaqui Pass Road, Borrego Springs; phone 619-824-1884.

Recommended Moderate and Budget Hotels

Coronado

CROWN CITY INN. Just blocks from the glamour of the Hotel del Coronado, but worlds away in terms of tariffs, this agreeable lodge features clean, newly decorated rooms, cable TV, a heated pool, and an on-site restaurant open for breakfast, lunch, and dinner. Within easy strolling distance of Coronado's major attractions, and just minutes by car from the San Diego Zoo and Sea World, the Crown City Inn has unbeatable rates. Rooms are $55 to $60, and a one-bedroom suite with kitchen is under $90.

520 Orange Avenue, Coronado; phone 619-435-6750.

VILLAGE INN. This delightful bed-and-breakfast, situated north of the Hotel del Coronado and just two blocks from the beach, is a real find, with ocean views, hardwood floors, four-poster beds, and private baths in its tastefully decorated, if somewhat small, guest rooms—all serviced by a rickety (but entirely safe) elevator. The complimentary Continental breakfasts can either be eaten in the kitchen or taken back to your room in a basket provided by Peter and Betsy Bogh, the hotel's proprietors and members of the family that has owned the building since the 1940s. The three-story structure, with its white walls, red-tile roof, ocean views, and ancient lift, is reminiscent of the Hotel del Coronado, but the rates are considerably cheaper. Rooms range from $50 to $90 a night, with breakfast included. On a recent holiday weekend, $64 would have gotten you a pleasant, second-story nook. The Village Inn is a perfect budget honeymoon spot or weekend retreat for lovers.

1017 Park Place, Coronado; phone 619-435-9318.

The Desert

PALM CANYON RESORT. Just steps away from the Anza Borrego Desert State Park Visitors Center, Palm Canyon Resort offers well-priced rooms and suites—some with in-room Jacuzzis—in its Territorial-style buildings. The 44 rooms here are spacious and simply but tastefully adorned. They have sitting areas and large, firm beds covered with chenille spreads. The property is spread out over 14 acres, although much of the space is taken up by the resort's RV park, which has room for 140 rigs.

Palm Canyon Resort has some nice amenities, including two heated pools and Jacuzzis and a nature library—perfect for brushing up on your zoology before you begin exploring the desert floor. Bicycles, four-wheel-drive vehicles, hiking tours, and stargazing outings are available for an extra fee. Las Palmas Bar and Grill, the hotel's restaurant, features Mexican dishes and outdoor dining.

Rates at Palm Canyon are $85 for a room without a balcony, $98 for a room with a balcony, and $125 for a suite with jacuzzi. Summer rates are about $30 to $40 less. The rate for the RV park, which includes cable TV, electricity, water, and sewer hookups, is $18. That drops to only $2 during the summer months.

221 Palm Canyon Drive, Borrego Springs; phone 619-767-5341.

Downtown

HOLIDAY INN HARBORVIEW. A centrally located inn with rooftop bar and restaurant and good views of the downtown skyline and Bay. Rooms are newly renovated and feature king or queen beds. Amenities include remote-control TV, free cable, and an outdoor heated pool. Rates are in the $60 to $80 range. There are no surprises here, just clean, convenient family-style accommodations.

1617 First Avenue, downtown; phone 619-233-6228.

ST. JAMES HOTEL. The St. James, San Diego's first sky-scraper, is well-priced and close to the San Diego Convention Center, the restaurants and nightlife offerings in the Gaslamp Quarter, and Horton Plaza. The 99 recently renovated rooms here have touches of Victoriana, and many have good views of the Bay. But the real treats are the rooftop garden and sundeck, which provide guests with a great view of the surrounding downtown area. Rooms here are in the $60 to $70 range. The downside is that this 100-year-old hotel has no parking of its own, and the hotel charges guests with cars $7.50 per day for the valet service. But, all in all, the St. James is a good spot, particularly for antiquarians and history buffs.

830 Sixth Avenue, downtown; phone 619-234-0155.

Old Town San Diego

HACIENDA HOTEL. This 150-suite Spanish colonial–revival inn, perched on a hill overlooking Old Town San Diego State Historic Park, is a moderately priced retreat surrounded by lushly landscaped grounds. Amenities include TVs with VCRs, in-room microwaves and refrigerators, a fitness center, on-site parking (good news here, because parking in Old Town can be a nightmare), two restaurants, and good views of the city and ocean. Rates are in the mid-$80s.

4041 Harney Street, San Diego; phone 619-298-4707.

Hotel Circle

TOWN AND COUNTRY HOTEL. The Town and Country has just emerged from a major refurbishment. Like all the hotels in Mission Valley's Hotel Circle, the Town and Country is centrally located, just minutes from the San Diego Zoo, Jack Murphy Stadium, and the beach.

But unlike some of its smaller rivals, the Town and Country also has a health club, four restaurants, four pools, and three lounges, as well as access to the neighboring golf course. The Sunday-morning brunch in the Gourmet Room, the hotel's main dining venue, is a not-to-be-missed delight. Rooms here are in the $95 range. Budget travelers note: The Town and Country's corporate owner, Atlas Hotels, also runs the neighboring Kings Inn and Mission Valley Inn, which offer guests rates in the $60 range as well as all privileges at Town and Country.

500 Hotel Circle North, San Diego; phone 619-291-7131.

SEVEN SEAS. This unpretentious Best Western lodge is just minutes from most attractions and provides guests with clean rooms, free parking, a 24-hour coffee shop, and round-the-clock room service. No major awards, no interesting history, but the rates can't be beat: $49 a night per couple. Kids stay for free.

411 Hotel Circle South, San Diego; phone 619-291-1300.

La Jolla

ANDREA VILLA INN. It doesn't have the La Jolla Beach and Tennis Club's private beach or putting green, but the Andrea Villa Inn does have a delightful tropical setting and moderately priced, nicely appointed rooms, all within blocks of La Jolla Shores Beach and the Scripps Aquarium. The rates here range from $60 for a large standard room to $95 for a suite. Amenities include heated pools and Jacuzzi and complimentary Continental breakfast.

2402 Torrey Pines Road, La Jolla; phone 619-459-3311.

Mexico

ROSARITO BEACH HOTEL. Since 1926, the Rosarito Beach Hotel has been welcoming guests who desire Southern California's Mediterranean climate without the region's madding crowds. Although the hotel deteriorated during the 1970s and early '80s, a recent renovation and addition have addressed most of the problems and brought the number of rooms up to nearly three hundred. Amenities here include tennis courts, racquetball courts, swimming pool, weekend floor shows in the bar, and, of course, spectacular beach frontage. Rooms start at $75 on weekends, but guests forty years of age and older enjoy a twenty percent discount on all rates.

HOTEL LAS ROCAS. A recent addition to Baja California's complement of hotels and inns, Las Rocas is a first-class hostelry, with 40 rooms and 34 suites, all tastefully decorated and quite comfortable. Suites have patios, fireplaces, refrigerators, wet bars, microwaves, and attractive reception areas. Amenities include two hot tubs, tennis courts, and a bar and restaurant. The hotel's spectacular pool is within splashing distance of the Pacific.

Rates range from $45 to $70, double occupancy. Suites fetch between $100 and $220. Continental breakfast for two is included in the weekend rate.

Chapter Eleven
♦♦♦♦♦♦♦♦♦♦♦

Shopping

BECAUSE San Diego County is essentially a collection of far-flung neighborhoods, fused together by a freeway system, it lacks the cohesive, pedestrian-oriented, central shopping districts you find in San Francisco, Seattle, and New York. The city's major department stores are located, with few exceptions, in shopping malls well outside the downtown urban core; most can only be reached by car or bus. Smaller boutiques and shops, selling handcrafted, one-of-a-kind, and distinctive items can be found throughout San Diego proper, but even these stores are most numerous in the old streetcar suburbs. For anyone who is downtown, the only malls readily accessible by foot are Horton Plaza and the Paladion. Prospect Street and Girard Avenue in La Jolla are a delight for strolling window-shoppers, but you'll need to drive or take a bus to get there.

Still, San Diego can be a great place to shop. Virtually every national retailer has at least two stores in the area, and a number of regional outfits have shops in malls in every corner of the county. And, of course, don't overlook shopping possibilities in neighboring Tijuana. Because Mexico has declared the entire Baja peninsula a free zone—waiving taxes on goods imported from outside the country—many European perfumes and some Japanese electronic goods can be had at bargain-basement prices. Tourists reentering the U.S. can bring back up to $400 worth of these foreign-made goods, tax-free. And because Mexico has been declared a "developing nation" under the General System of Preferences (GSP), all duties on goods made in Mexico are waived.

Shopping Areas

Adams Avenue, which begins in University Heights and runs east to Kensington, paralleling El Cajon Boulevard, is home to San Diego's antique district, with two dozen shops scattered down its length selling vintage furnishings and accessories. The largest concentrations of these stores are in Normal Heights and Kensington, two streetcar suburbs, where the old shops have been saved from destruction by the mom-and-pop antique operations. There are other shops and cafes on Adams Avenue worth checking out, including the Incredible Cheesecake Company, The Kensington Coffee Company, and the Ken Cinema (see page 200).

Avenida Revolución, the center for shopping in Tijuana, has been throughly transformed of late. Once the coarse main drag of that city (though by no means as bawdy as the *Zona Norte*), today Revolución is, for the most part, an attractive shopping area, offering designer fashions, interesting specialty shops, and a number of good restaurants. Popular stores here include Maxim, Sara (imported apparel and perfumes), Tolan (Mexican folk art and furnishings), and Azteca (gold jewelry). Ralph Lauren and Guess also have shops on the avenue.

Bazaar Del Mundo (2754 Calhoun Street, Old Town; 296-3161), with its Spanish-style architecture, is a former motor court that has been lovingly transformed into a colorful showplace and bustling shopping spot for traditional and contemporary Mexican pottery, curios, and folk art. The inner courtyard, ringed by shops, restaurants, and bars, periodically features live costumed entertainment. Artes de Mexico and The Design Center Interiors are perhaps the Bazaar's most interesting shops, featuring housewares and home furnishings with an ethnic flair. Casa de Pico, Bazaar Del Mundo's Mexican eatery, serves margaritas big enough to swim in.

Del Shops are 28 specialty stores located in the Victorian wing of the magnificent Hotel del Coronado. The stores sell everything from Hummel figurines to designer clothing to fine art and jewelry. There's even an authentic Jewish delicatessen, the Del Deli, operating out of what used to be the hotel's cistern. The shops provide a good excuse to come to Coronado and a fine way to start a tour of the hotel.

Little Italy is, unfortunately, living up to its name, becoming tinier and tinier every day. At press time, it was located on India Street, between Cedar and Fern, but it could be even smaller by the time you arrive. The restaurants and bakeries here offer magnificent prosciutto, delicious pistachio cakes, and hearty breads—perfect for picnicking.

Prospect Street in La Jolla has designer boutiques, including Polo, as well as art galleries, cafes, bars, and restaurants, and it's one of the few pedestrian-friendly shopping districts in the county. Although on-street parking is a nightmare, merchants here validate parking with purchases. Prospect is the undisputed main drag, but Girard Avenue is worth exploring as well, with Roche-Bobois, Saks Fifth Avenue, I. Magnin, and numerous fashionable boutiques—including the Ascot Shop, a locally-renowned men's clothier—and home accessory shops along its length.

Shopping Centers

Golden Triangle is a high-density shopping and business district with three large malls located within its boundaries: Costa Verde (8650 Genesee Avenue, 458-9270); La Jolla Village Square (8657 Villa La Jolla Drive, 455-7550); and University Towne Center (4500 La Jolla Village Drive, 546-8858). Of the three, University Towne Center (UTC) and La Jolla Village Square are to be preferred, in that order. UTC is a sprawling mall with Nordstrom, Robinson's, Broadway, and Sears Roebuck department stores, a movie theater, a food court, a skating rink, a very good Japanese restaurant, and even a museum—the Mingei International Museum of Folk Art (453-5300). La Jolla Village Square is home to the May Company, Bullock's Wilshire, Trader Joe's, and one of the few remaining Piret's bistros (see page 144). The Children's Museum (450-0767) is also located here, offering hands-on creative experiences for the kids. (It's a pity the curators won't permit parents to leave their children here while they shop.) In between UTC and La Jolla Village Square is the Aventine, an office and hotel development designed by Robert Graves.

Horton Plaza (Broadway and Fourth Avenue, downtown; 238-1596) is an airy, six-level mall with a playful pastiche of architectural motifs incorporated into its six-and-a-half-block design. The shops here tend to be part of national chains, including Nordstrom, Broadway, Eddie Bauer, Jaeger, Ann Taylor, The Nature Company, Doubleday, and Williams-Sonoma. There's also an Omni Hotel on the west side of the plaza, a seven-screen theater complex on the east side, and a number of convenient noshing spots in between. The Farmers Market at the far end of the mall is a gourmet's delight, with the best meat case and most exotic vegetable selection in town and a tempting array of takeout treats perfect for picnickers. Horton Plaza is also the home of the San Diego Repertory Theatre, which mounts its productions on two underground stages next to Robinson's. A nominal fee is charged for parking in the adjacent lot, but retailers in the mall validate. If you're not interested in shopping, Horton Plaza still is worth a look, if only to see how its architects attempted to blend the brand-new mall into the older neighborhood surrounding it. The cafe at Nordstrom, which offers a satisfying and quite reasonable blue-plate special each day, has an outdoor patio with a good view west, toward the convention center and Bay.

Mission Valley and *Fashion Valley* together have more than 180 shops between them, including major department stores, smaller boutiques, and a handful of restaurants. Mission Valley (1640 Camino Del Rio North, alongside Interstate 8 in Mission Valley; 296-6375) is home to Bullock's, Saks Fifth Avenue, Brooks Brothers, and May Company, as well as a number of specialty stores. Fashion Valley (just west of the Friars Road exit on state Route 163, Mission Valley; 297-3381) has Nordstrom, Neiman Marcus, Johnston & Murphy, Robinson's, and J. C. Penney as well as Pottery Barn and Crate and Barrel—two popular home-furnishings outlets.

North County Fair (272 East Via Rancho Parkway, Escondido; 489-2332) is the county's largest shopping mall, anchored by no less than six major department stores—May Company, Nordstrom, Robinson's, Sears, The Broadway, and J. C. Penney—and some 170 specialty shops. Because it's right down the road from the San Diego Wild Animal Park (234-6541), the 2,000-acre exotic-wildlife preserve run by the San Diego Zoo, North County Fair is a good spot to begin a daylong shopping safari.

Old Ferry Landing (1201 First Avenue, Coronado; 435-8895) is where you'll disembark if you take the Coronado—San Diego Ferry across the Bay (see page 58). This waterfront mall has a handful of specialty shops and restaurants and a good view of downtown San Diego. Boat owners who ferry themselves here can tie up at free boat slips.

Paladion (777 Front Street, downtown; 234-1891), located just west of Horton Plaza, has a number of well-known, high-end retailers, including Tiffany & Co., Gucci, Alfred Dunhill, and Cartier, selling jewelry, apparel, and home accessories. The indoor atrium is a pleasant spot for a snack, but the cafe on Nordstrom's third floor (next door at Horton Plaza) boasts a much better view and easier-to-swallow prices.

Plaza Rio Tijuana (Corner of Avenida Independencia and Paseo de los Heroes, Tijuana; 011-52-66-840402) has Sears, Dorian's (a rather fine department store), specialty shops, leather designers, and a multiscreen theater, which screens films in English with Spanish subtitles. This is a nice place to take advantage of Mexico's many bargains without dealing with the crowded scene on Avenida Revolución.

San Diego Factory Outlet Center (4498 Camino de la Plaza, San Ysidro; 690-2999) has 24 factory-direct outlet stores, discounting everything from Levi jeans, Bass footwear, Corningware cookware, and Nike sneakers to Black & Decker power tools and Izod/Gant and Eddie Bauer sportswear.

Seaport Village (Kettner Boulevard and Harbor Drive, downtown; 235-4013) is a 15-acre "festival market," not unlike Manhattan's South Street Seaport or San Francisco's Pier 39. The architecture is far more reminiscent of a New England fishing village than old San Diego, and many of the sixty-odd "shoppes" are undistinguished. But this fanciful cityscape is a big hit with visitors and locals, perhaps because of its location right alongside the harbor. Candy emporia, gift shops, kite dealers, a California store, and a turn-of-the-century carousel—restored and running—take up most of the complex, but there are also a number of restaurants here. Your kids may like the mimes, jugglers, and clowns who stroll throughout the village.

Specialty Shops

Bookstar (3150 Rosecrans Place, Point Loma; 225-0465) is San Diego's largest and most comprehensive discount bookstore. Set in the old Loma Theater, which has been playfully restored, Bookstar is a reader's delight, with a good selection of fiction and nonfiction works and with benches set up by the hefty magazine racks to accommodate browsers.

Farmers Bazaar (215 Seventh Avenue, downtown; 233-0281) is a high-energy, multilingual fruit, flower, vegetable, and seafood market, popular with budget-minded shoppers and restaurateurs. It's a good place to stop for a healthy snack when you tour the Gaslamp Quarter.

International Gallery (643 G Street, downtown; 235-8255) sells cultural curiosities and religious icons unearthed from places as diverse as Nigeria, Syria, and Turkey, as well as textiles, pottery, and jewelry from around the world. The proprietors periodically offer tours to destinations like Turkey, Egypt, Tunisia, and Pakistan, for travelers who share their interest in the exotic.

Nordstrom (Fashion Valley, Horton Plaza, University Towne Center, and North County Fair) is, to many minds, the most sophisticated retailer in the city. The Seattle-based store offers top-of-the-line custom and off-the-rack apparel, friendly and attentive service, and a no-questions-asked return policy. If you're looking for bargains, there's also a Nordstrom Rack in town, just west of Mission Valley Center (824 Camino Del Rio North, Mission Valley; 296-0143).

Padres/Chargers Gift Shops (Jack Murphy Stadium, 9449 Friars Road, Mission Valley; 584-7200) features officially sanctioned National Football League and Major League Baseball items, including the jerseys, jackets, hats, batting helmets, and more, of San Diego's football and baseball franchises, the Chargers and the Padres.

St. Vincent de Paul Specialty Store (4574 Park Boulevard, University Heights; 233-8797) is an upscale thrift store filled with unwanted knickknacks, clothing, and furnishings from some of San Diego's best households. During the last weekend of every month, prices are discounted twenty percent. The nice thing here is that the proceeds benefit the St. Vincent de Paul Homeless Shelter, a facility built by McDonald's owner Joan Kroc that provides temporary quarters and a lasting dose of dignity to families and individuals making the difficult trek back home.

Sausage King (811 W. Washington Street, Mission Hills; 297-4301) is a German-run delicatessen with the second-best meat case in the county. (The best is at the Horton Plaza Farmers Market.) A huge assortment of sausages are on sale here, along with delightful hard rolls, real German potato salad, and interesting condiments. It's a good place to stop on your way to that picnic in Presidio Park—especially if you have a hibachi in tow.

Swap Meet

Kobey's Swap Meet happens every Thursday through Sunday in the parking lot of the San Diego Sports Arena.

Hundreds of professional and amateur vendors transform the lot into an open-air bazaar, hawking everything from antique furnishings to brand-name swimsuits and electronics to the thousands of shoppers who pass through the turnstiles. Call 226-0650 for more information.

Chapter Twelve
♦♦♦♦♦♦♦♦♦♦♦

Entertainment

SAN DIEGANS may be noted for their easygoing lifestyles and laid-back ways. But they take their entertainment very seriously indeed.

Of course, San Diego isn't New York, and if you're in the city for any length of time, you'll undoubtedly over-hear people going on about the sad state of the city's cultural scene or lamenting the indifference of San Di-egans to culture.

Ignore them. Insiders know better.

Although some of San Diego's aspiring artists do indeed skip town and head north to Los Angeles, many of the city's very best performing professionals never leave. On any given night, topnotch entertainers can be found at bars, cafés, nightclubs, concert halls, and theaters around town, playing to crowds that are sometimes rowdy, some-times reserved, but rarely apathetic.

It's easy to see why. From raucous lounges in down-town, where overflow crowds spill out onto the street, to subdued piano bars in La Jolla, where progressive jazz provides the background music for power chats, San

Diego offers enough entertainment options to satisfy anyone's shifting moods.

And, because nationally and internationally acclaimed performers are as eager as anyone else to bask in the legendary San Diego sunshine, the calendar here is filled with performing arts events year-round. Whether you want high culture or low, San Diego has what you're looking for.

For the most up-to-date information on evening amusements, check the *Reader*, a free weekly tabloid distributed on Thursdays, or the "Night & Day" section of the Thursday *San Diego Union-Tribune*. Both offer an extensive listing of clubs, concerts, and events. Better yet, call the venues themselves for the most current news. For all numbers listed below, the area code is 619.

Nightclubs and Bars

San Diego's spirited mixture of fun is especially abundant in the downtown area, where many of the city's hottest nightspots and sophisticated dance clubs are concentrated.

Downtown's Gaslamp Quarter, which somewhat ingenuously bills itself as "The Historic Heart of San Diego," is nonetheless a good place to start, with a number of reliable spots for dancing, drinking, and relaxing.

During the past several years, a handful of gutsy restaurateurs and tavern keepers have created what millions of dollars in redevelopment money and a battalion of civic boosters never could: a Gaslamp Quarter that shines, especially at night. The variety here is amazing—particularly on weekends—and most of it comes without a cover charge. Unfortunately, the neighborhood still has something of an "edge," so newcomers are advised to visit with friends after dark. You should have no qualms however, about touring the area during the day.

If you're happiest in crowded places, try Cafe Sevilla at 555 Fourth Avenue (233-5979) or Ole Madrid Cafe at 751 Fifth Avenue (557-0146). Both serve up fun with a serious single-mindedness. Though the two restaurants reserve plenty of room for dedicated drinkers, they also offer a wonderful variety of Spanish appetizers, or *tapas*, at very reasonable prices. You can sip on ambrosial sangria, or snack on *tortilla* (a wonderful egg and potato omelet unlike the Mexican staple of the same name), while enjoying traditional Iberian exuberance.

For those who like their nightlife on the jazzy side, Croce's at 802 Fifth Avenue (233-4355) is an option close in. Owned and operated by Ingrid Croce, Jim's widow, Croce's offers up some of the swingingest jazz in the area. West Coast, New Orleans, Chicago, and Kansas City styles of jazz are all at home here, as is A. J. Croce, Jim's son, who stops by several nights a week to play with friends. A bonus at Croce's is that the music starts early, often around 5 P.M., making it easy for the early-to-bed crowd to enjoy the fun.

If you're willing to leave downtown in search of jazz, try Elario's, atop the Summer House Inn (see page 155). Things are a bit more formal and elegant than at Croce's, and there's often a cover charge. But Elario's still swings, thanks to aggressive booking and spectacular ocean views. Recent concerts here have featured the likes of Sheila Jordan, Jimmy McGriff, and Hermeto Pascoal. More subdued, and closer to downtown, is the piano bar at Mister A's (see page 154). Jackets are required, but the sumptuous surroundings and panoramic views of the downtown skyline are worth the effort. Elario's and Mister A's are comfortable, intimate rooms, attracting a slightly more mature crowd, but young professionals are beginning to frequent both spots.

Around the corner from Croce's is Patrick's II at 428 F Street (233-3077). The Gaslamp Quarter has experienced some very dark periods over the years, but through them all Patrick's II has shined, providing great music and warm hospitality in a cellar-like setting. Despite its Irish-sounding moniker, Patrick's II features entertainment of the American kind, heavy on rhythm and blues and Dixieland. On Wednesday and Thursday nights, music is provided by Fro Brigham's Preservation Band, a group of (mostly) octogenarians that swings like a gang of hormone-addled youngsters. Although you'd never know it from the size of the dance floor, this brick-lined nook does indeed have a cabaret license, and patrons are invited to cut the rug. Patrick's II is timelessly hip and absolutely free, though possibly a little *too* loud if you're merely looking for background music.

Another downtown possibility is Karl Strauss's Old Columbia Brewery and Grill at 1157 Columbia Street (234-2739), a pub that offers some interesting beers crafted right on the premises. It's a bit of a walk from the Gaslamp Quarter, and the interior design is somewhat austere, but if you're a fan of microbreweries, it's worth the trek. There's no live music at Old Columbia, but there's plenty of live entertainment, most of it provided by patrons who try to down the enormous schooners of beer on sale here. As San Diego's first brew pub, and with its location near City Hall, Old Columbia has become an afterwork institution for local politicians and power brokers.

For shaggier types, the best nightspot in town is probably the Casbah, at 2812 Kettner Boulevard (294-9033). Owned by Tim Maze, a former concert promoter, this dark, smoky club is a favorite hangout for San Diego's smoldering youth. Weekly events include the angst-ridden "Acoustic Hell," when the club's microphones are commandeered by young hopefuls who belt out impassioned versions of their favorite songs and look belligerent. There's often a cover charge on Friday and Saturday, but the weekend shows usually bring respectable up-and-coming bands and refreshing new faces to the Casbah's small stage.

The tiny Alibi at 1403 University Avenue (295-0881) draws an odd mixture of hipsters and pensioners who apparently share an appreciation of dark settings, cheap drinks, pool tables, and easygoing chatter. As the word has spread about this hole-in-the-wall, and as the lines outside have grown, some of the Alibi's regulars have relocated to the Lamplighter, a Mission Hills joint at 817 W. Washington Street. The clientele is again eclectic and the jukebox, arguably the best in the city, reflects that diversity, featuring Sinatra, Fats Domino, The Clash, Willie Nelson, and Dave Brubeck. Fortunately, the volume is kept at a moderate level and conversation is never forced to take a back seat to the music.

Two newer saloons, both just outside the downtown area, are gaining fans. Live Wire, a fun and frothy drafthouse at 2103 El Cajon Boulevard (291-7450), is the newer of the two. The suds at Live Wire, which range from Miller to Pete's Wicked Ale, are available only on draft. Cappuccino and espresso are available as well. The tunes, courtesy of a 300-watt CD jukebox, range widely and suit the bar's wildly mixed crowd of regulars. Friendly games of eight ball dominate Live Wire's back section; conversation is the preferred game up front.

Shakespeare's Pub and Grille, at 3701 India Street (299-0230), is another good choice for premium-beer lovers. It offers a variety of English and Irish brews—and well-priced pub grub—in a setting that's pretty close to the real thing. Shakespeare's is recommended for Anglophiles of all ages.

A final option, back in the Gaslamp Quarter, is Bodies at 528 F Street (236-8988). Before it closed in the early 1980s, the original Bodies on El Cajon Boulevard helped bring the Beat Farmers and wildman Mojo Nixon to national attention. At its roomy new location, the club continues the tradition, keeping Top 40 and heavy-metal bands at arm's length and spotlighting original American music, including rockabilly and rhythm and blues, in an honest, intimate beer-bar setting. Bodies is quickly eclipsing other venues around town as the premier showcase for local bands with crunching guitar riffs, gritty vocals, and high hopes.

San Diego's beach areas offer visitors plenty of possibilities for daytime recreation; the good news these days is that the fun continues into the night. Although they used to roll up the streets—and shake out the sand—at sunset just a few years ago, the number of worthwhile nightclubs in the area has steadily increased since the early 1980s, when a host of new spots sprung up, displacing some of the older, decaying gin mills.

The hands-down favorite for relaxing fun in the area is the Cass Street Bar and Grill at 4612 Cass Street in Pacific Beach (270-1320), where the atmosphere is frank and friendly. On warm days, the sidewalk windows open up, providing patrons with an unobstructed view of passersby. Although Cass Street has no live entertainment, visitors can enjoy a congenial game of miniature shuffleboard with the regulars (whose skill at the game suggests they may have a little *too* much time on their hands). The conversation here revolves around waves and women, the Chargers and the Padres, but still provides a nice entrée into the laid-back, lollygagging side of San Diego.

Blind Melons, at 710 Garnet Avenue in Pacific Beach (483-7844), showcases live reggae and R&B every night. The Jazz Note, at 860 Garnet Avenue in Pacific Beach (272-1832), offers jazz on weekends. Both charge a cover, which varies.

If you're in La Jolla and in the mood to relax and watch the world go by, Alfonso's, at 1251 Prospect Avenue (454-2232), and Jose's Courtroom, at 1037 Prospect Avenue (454-7655), provide perfect perches for lounging and gawking. Alfonso's has an especially delightful front patio, close to the busy sidewalk, giving you a front seat on La Jolla's main drag. When you're ready to move on, try the Hard Rock Cafe's unique blend of off-the-rack activism and loud fun, just down the street at 909 Prospect Avenue (454-5101).

If your tastes run to the bizarre, try Pacific Shores, at 4927 Newport Avenue in Ocean Beach (223-7549), or the Nite Owl, at 2772 Garnet Avenue in Pacific Beach (276-3933). Pac Shores is easily the stranger of the two. From the outside, it appears to be a standard neighborhood bar. Step inside, and you enter a world where David Lynch meets Lawrence Welk. Drinks at this cross-generational favorite are remarkably cheap and the patrons quite friendly. Unless one of the older regulars drops his teeth, the only rowdiness comes during the weekends, when students from a nearby religious college stop in and try to gain spiritual insight by chug-a-lugging beer. No major "improvements" have been made to the bar in years, so Pac Shores offers a *noir* atmosphere that is missing in so many of the newer theme bars around town.

For live music in the beach area, try the Belly Up Tavern at 143 S. Cedros Avenue in Solana Beach (481-9022). Although it's a good twenty-minute drive up the coast from downtown, this barn-like club regularly attracts some of the nation's top acts. Only Sound FX, formerly the Bacchanal, at 8022 Clairemont Mesa Boulevard in Kearny Mesa can hold a lighter to it. The wonderful thing about the Belly Up Tavern is its owners' willingness to reinvent the club every night of the week. Swing, big-band, zydeco, reggae, folk, and rock-and-roll acts—and their fans—are all welcome at the club and performers as diverse as the Duke Ellington Orchestra, the Desert Rose Band, and the Red Hot Chile Peppers have appeared on the stage. For a quieter evening, try one of the Belly Up's early-evening shows, featuring local Dixieland, swing, and country bands.

Closer to downtown, in Ocean Beach, the Texas Teahouse, at 4970 Voltaire Street, and Winston's, at 1921 Bacon Street, are steady, dependable spots for beer-bar rock and dive-bar ambience. Tom "Cat" Courtney, a legendary session guitarist who recorded with the likes of T-Bone Walker and Jimmy Reed before moving to San Diego in the mid-1970s, is a regular attraction at both clubs.

Dancing

San Diego has a number of clubs where patrons can dance to a Top 40 soundtrack. By all accounts, one of the best is Confetti, at 5373 Mission Center Road in Mission Valley (291-8635). You'll have a dress code and a cover charge to contend with here, but the dance complex is huge, with flashy lighting and the trademark "club" sound. The accent at the nightclub is on loud music and suggestive dancing, but the periodic flurries of confetti in the vicinity of the dance floor—hence the club's name—work to keep things playful.

Two other centrally located dance clubs are the Red Onion, at 3125 Ocean Front Walk in Mission Beach (488-9040), and Club Emerald City, at 945 Garnet Avenue in Pacific Beach (483-9920). Both attract young singles and offer a varied mix of music. In Hillcrest, just up the hill from downtown, the Arena, at 308 University Avenue, and Rick's, at 1051 University Avenue, are dance spots favored by young gays but increasingly popular with straights as well.

In recent years, San Diego has witnessed an explosion in the number of roving "underground" nightclubs where the clientele dances to bass-heavy mixes of funk, disco, and house music. The records are spun by skilled deejays, the dancing is wild and outrageous, and the atmosphere is sweaty but fun. The Kansas City Steak House, at 535 Fifth Avenue (557-0525), and Sibyl's Down Under, at 500 Fourth Avenue (239-9117), seem to host these affairs regularly, but because locations change so frequently it's best to consult the *Reader* for up-to-date information.

Coffeehouses

Although a recent study revealed that the average San Diegan spends a staggering $465 a year on liquor, many locals, looking for alternatives to the bar scene, have rediscovered the simple joy of coffee and coffeehouses. Long a mecca for poets, punks, and professors, local java joints are beginning to attract a more varied public. A few pattern themselves on the cafes of Europe, but most of the city's coffee emporia seem to take their cues from the coffeehouses of beatnik San Francisco and folksy Greenwich Village. All offer powerfully good brews, caffeinated chatter, and the warm hissing sound of the espresso machine.

The largest concentration of coffeehouses can be found on the fringes of the Gaslamp Quarter. One of the first, and still one of the most popular, is the gallery-like Java, at 837 G Street (235-4012). Java offers patrons a cool, contemporary space and a wonderful variety of pulse-quickening brews. Try the intriguingly sweet, wonderfully cool Vietnamese coffee here. If you'd like the option of ordering alcohol, Cafe Lulu, at 419 F Street (238-0114), features both wine and coffee—and a truly bizarre interior. Cafe Chabalaba, at 1070 16th Avenue, is an agreeable though noisy newcomer to the coffee-shop scene. Smoking is banned here but music isn't, and Chabalaba rings late into the night with live entertainment. If you prefer a more contemplative setting, Seventh Near B, at

1146 Seventh Avenue (696-7071), offers a variety of coffees and teas and a good assortment of newspapers and magazines from around the world. But get there early: Seventh Near B closes at 7 P.M.

In Hillcrest, try Quel Fromage, at 523 University Avenue (295-1600), which attracts down-at-the-heel grad students from UCSD and folks with dog-eared copies of impenetrable novels who aren't officially registered anywhere. The Soho Tea and Coffee Shop, just down the street at 1417 University Avenue (299-7646), stays open until 4 A.M. and does a busy after-bar business. At the northernmost edge of what once was San Diego's "Little Italy," just west of Mission Hills, there's Gelato Vera, at 3751 India Street (454-8977). Few Italian-Americans live here now, but Gelato Vera is the sort of café that was a fixture in the old neighborhood. The lines can be long here, but the espresso, cappuccino, and Italian ice creams are worth the wait. On warm evenings, check out the screened-in patio on the café's second floor.

Comedy

A number of venues around town occasionally offer comedy, but only four or five clubs in the city are dedicated to the art, featuring professional comedians on a regular basis. As it happens, most of the clubs are in the beach area, making club-hopping convenient and easy.

The Comedy Store South, at 916 Pearl Street in La Jolla (454-9176) is the oldest, but the Improv Comedy Cafe, at 832 Garnet Avenue (483-4520), has the best reputation among aficionados. Both clubs have a cover charge, a two-drink minimum, and lines running down the block, but at the Improv you can skip the queue entirely by paying an extra $10. For that price, you're immediately seated at a good table and served the entrée of your choice from a limited but reliable menu. (Same-day advance reservations are recommended for this option.) Again, check the *Reader* for performers and dates.

Another solid spot for comedy in the city is the Comedy Isle, inside the Bahia Hotel at 998 West Mission Bay Drive in Mission Beach (488-6872). In North County, your only option is Comedy Nite, at 2216 El Camino Real, Oceanside, a waypoint for comedians traveling between San Diego and Los Angeles that is beginning to draw big names.

For fans of bizarre, off-the-wall comedy, the Ken Cinema at 4061 Adams Avenue in Kensington (283-5909) periodically offers a treat, screening old B movies with brand-new, ad-libbed dialogue courtesy of a Los Angeles-based improvisational comedy troupe. The effect is similar to the one achieved by Woody Allen in *What's Up, Tiger Lily?*, but at the Ken it's done without benefit of rehearsal. The result is ninety minutes of unpredictable, inspired fun bordering on pure anarchy.

Speaking of film and comedy, the Festival of Animation passes through San Diego each year, stopping for a few weeks to screen its delightful cartoon shorts at the San Diego Museum of Contemporary Art, at 700 Prospect Street in La Jolla (551-9274). Although weekend shows tend to sell out early, good seats for weekday screenings are normally available on the day of the show. Advance tickets are available from Ticketmaster (278-TIXS).

Theater

A few years ago, when August Wilson was looking for a receptive, sophisticated audience to help put the finishing touches to a new play he'd penned, the Pulitzer- and Tony-winning writer premiered the work in San Diego. The locals loved it. So did the critics. The story illustrates an important point: While Los Angeles may have a firm grip on its title as the film capital of the United States, San Diego has quietly developed a reputation for its passionate appreciation of legitimate theater.

It's a passion San Diegans have acquired watching the talent and professionalism of local performers. Although the city's eight legitimate theater companies can, and often do, call on nationally known actors and actresses to round out their casts, they draw most of their energy and inspiration from local performers, playwrights, and producers.

In addition to staging fine adaptations of Shakespeare, San Diego's Old Globe Theater mounts some of the best original play series anywhere. Whether you're looking for comedy with an edgy relevance or more ponderous pieces with Themes and Subtexts jumping out of the scenery, the Globe is always reliable. The summer series under the stars is a local favorite, but the winter season at the Carter Center Stage is enjoyable as well. For 24-hour ticket information, call the Old Globe at 234-5623 or stop by the ticket office inside Balboa Park, just behind the magnificent California Building.

The San Diego Repertory Theatre, which used to stage its plays in the converted chapel of an old funeral home on Sixth Avenue, has settled into its spacious new digs at Horton Plaza (235-8025). The company's director, Sam Woodhouse, has a taste for the outrageous, but he squeezes solid, thought-provoking work out of his resourceful troupe. Comedy is, however, the group's strong suit.

In addition to the Rep, several distinguished companies mount quality work around the city throughout the year, including the Bowery Theatre at the Kingston Playhouse, the Gaslamp Quarter Theatre, and Sledgehammer Theatre, which operates out of the Rep's old digs at 1620 Sixth Avenue. Check the *Reader* for current plays and showtimes.

The La Jolla Playhouse, founded in 1947 by Gregory Peck and Dorothy McGuire to give Hollywood actors a chance to do theater work without schlepping back to New York, is an often overlooked theatrical gem in San Diego. Des McAnuff, the company's director, earned a Tony Award in 1984 with *Big River*, and he's continued to stage ambitious projects with the group. The La Jolla Playhouse is at 2910 La Jolla Village Drive, at the southern end of the UCSD campus (534-3960).

For theatergoers who find themselves in San Diego, the great news is that day-of-the-show half-price tickets are now available for most shows from Arts Tix. Unfortunately, credit cards are not accepted and tickets must be picked up in person from the Arts Tix kiosk (238-3810), in front of Horton Plaza and across the street from the U.S. Grant Hotel.

If you're in the mood for something a little more experimental, try the Sushi Performance Gallery at 852 Eighth Avenue, downtown. Sushi is San Diego's premier performance-art space, presenting a variety of semispontaneous monologues and mini-dramas by well-known and up-and-coming artists and raconteurs. Some observers complain that the taxpayer-supported types who appear here are more interested in gutter politics than street theater, but Sushi does make a real effort to attract a good number of inventive, if slightly traumatized, performance-art pros. The gallery's annual month-long NeoFest has become something of a spring rite locally. Recent performers have included Eric Bogosian, David Cale, and Rhodessa Jones. When Sushi isn't hosting a performance piece, the gallery displays works by local artists. Call 235-8466 for information.

San Diego unfortunately remains a second-tier touring

stop for Broadway shows, but popular musicals like *Les Miserables*, *Cats*, and *Grand Hotel* eventually do get here. Copley Symphony Hall, at 1245 Seventh Avenue (699-4200), and the Civic Theatre at 202 C Street (236-6510), normally host these gala stage presentations. Tickets for these shows also are available from the San Diego Playgoers (231-8995).

Classical Music and Opera

Since it was founded in 1927, the San Diego Symphony Orchestra has provided the city with an annual schedule of exciting concerts. Although the group hit some sour notes during the 1980s, a new contract and a new home seem to have improved matters. David Atherton, the colorful former conductor, now waves his baton in Hong Kong during most of the year, but the Symphony continues to move forward under music director Yoav Talmi, recording, touring, and playing to a growing group of fans from the stage at Copley Symphony Hall, at 1245 Seventh Avenue (699-4205). The group's summer concert series (see "Seasonal Offerings," below) at the Embarcadero Marina, which features fireworks, is especially popular, but the regular season is beginning to attract great interest. Although they outrage snobs, Talmi's preconcert remarks provide a nice introduction to the evening's music. The Symphony also offers a Nickelodeon Series during the year, screening silent-movie classics with live pipe-organ accompaniment. Past shows have featured *Phantom of the Opera* and *The Thief of Baghdad*.

The annual Mostly Mozart Festival brings an accomplished ensemble into the city each June, including former maestro David Atherton, who acts as the program's musical director. The emphasis during the two-week festival is on Mozart, naturally, but the works of Bach, Schubert, Beethoven, and Haydn usually get an airing as well.

The Civic Theatre, at 202 C Street (236-6510), is also home to the San Diego Opera, which has become quite ambitious under its new boss, Ian Campbell. The company's season runs from fall through spring. Recent offerings have included Mozart's *Cosi fan tutte*, Benjamin Britten's *Albert Herring*, Strauss's *Die Fledermaus*, and Carlisle Floyd's *Passion of Jonathon Wade*.

Seasonal Offerings

Not surprisingly, San Diego's annual entertainment calendar is filled with many of the same events and holidays celebrated in other cities around the country. In the weeks leading up to Christmas, for instance, local boat owners deck their vessels with festive lights and stage a dazzling nighttime parade on the Bay, an event many San Diegans view from the shore. The Symphony and Pops Orchestras also offer an annual festival of holiday concerts and performances, many of which are free and highly recommended. Another seasonal favorite for San Diegans of all ethnic groups is *Cinco de Mayo*, the annual celebration commemorating Mexico's declaration of independence. Festivities are held on May 5 throughout San Diego. The most popular of these is the fiesta held in Old Town. If you choose Old Town's Cinco de Mayo, go early: Although a promised trolley extension should eventually relieve the congestion, parking in the area remains tight and many folks come early and leave late to catch all the color.

San Diego's yearly Oktoberfest bash in Balboa Park is also great fun, but it simply can't compare to the festivities held in neighboring La Mesa, where the city fathers seal off the streets and transform their quiet downtown into a giant, rollicking beer garden. Best of all, you can join the thousands of revelers without ever getting behind the wheel of your car. Just hop on the San Diego Trolley's East Line, get off at La Mesa Boulevard, and yell "Prosit!"

If there is one season when San Diego truly comes alive, it's summer. The average evening temperature hovers in the low 70s and a number of venues around town take advantage of the balmy nights to host outdoor concert series. The following is an overview of these offerings; the *Reader* or Thursday *San Diego Union-Tribune* will have up-to-date information.

For folks who combine a love of nature with a passion for jazz, there's Humphrey's Half Moon Inn, at 2241 Shelter Island Drive (224-3577). During recent summer series here, Harry Connick, Dave Brubeck, Harry Belafonte, and Ray Charles have played on Humphrey's waterfront stage. The only drawback to this airy, good-spirited venue is that there is a comprehensive no-smoking policy on the grounds. Still, smokers are encouraged to give it a try. The music and setting are so relaxing you may surprise yourself and find that you don't need a cigarette.

Another outdoor possibility is provided by the San Diego Symphony's SummerPops concert series by the Bay. Two years ago, the annual event was moved from Mission Bay's Hospitality Point to the Embarcadero Marina to escape the noise of jets taking off from nearby Lindbergh Field. It was, by all accounts, a change for the better, and concertgoers can now appreciate the free early-evening shows and the memorable music they celebrate. Call the Symphony at 699-4205 for information.

Perhaps the best summer concert spot is the Open Air Amphitheatre at San Diego State University (594-6947). The surroundings are not quite as dramatic as those at Humphrey's, but the Open Air's summer lineup tends to offer more variety. Often, things are as entertaining outside the amphitheater as they are inside—and much cheaper to boot. On any given night, hundreds of thrifty folks throw blankets down on the grass surrounding the theater and picnic, chat, and listen to the musicians who play, unseen, on the stage. Past series have featured Elvis Costello, Joe Jackson, Gipsy Kings, and George Benson. It's a cheap way to enjoy some of the best performers who pass through town and a delightful opportunity to meet San Diegans who share your impeccable sense of value.

If you're lucky enough to be in the city in early September, consider stopping by the Street Scene. This annual two-day event brings traffic in the Gaslamp Quarter to a halt, as reggae, gospel, rockabilly, Tex-Mex, blues, zydeco, worldbeat, and, yes, even polka performers occupy one of the five stages set up for the event. Since it began in the early 1980s, the Street Scene has experienced an explosion in popularity. Today, it ranks as the city's largest mass-participation event and underscores how very serious and sweeping the entertainment scene is in San Diego.

Annual Events

OVER-THE-LINE TOURNAMENT: This annual competition on Mission Bay's Fiesta Island is a spectacular display of San Diego–style beach madness. Tens of thousands of party-animal spectators guzzle beers while hundreds of teams—most with unprintable names—play a three-man softball game said to have originated in Mission Beach during the 1940s. The idea is to hit the ball 55 feet, or "over-the-line." Each player is allowed only one strike before being called out. After three outs, the teams switch positions. Success on the field is important, but most participants seem to put most of their energy into devising sexually explicit team names and creating complicated headgear that permits them to drink beer while they play. It's a grand display of six-pack decadence. Bring sunscreen, lawn chairs, and plenty of your favorite beverage. Mid-July. 297-8480.

DEL MAR THOROUGHBRED RACING SEASON: Since it was founded in 1937 by Bing Crosby and Pat O'Brien, the Del Mar Racetrack has become one of America's premier thoroughbred racing tracks. Notable events here have included Seabiscuit's $25,000, winner-take-all victory over Ligaroti in 1938 and Willie Shoemaker's 6,033rd win. During the season, which runs from late July to mid-September, the club attracts a delightful cross-section of San Diegans who love colorful silks, the thrill of the home-stretch, and the promise of pari-mutuel betting. To this day, Crosby's "Where the Turf Meets the Surf" is broad-cast over the racetrack's loudspeakers before the first and after the ninth race every day except Tuesday, when the track is closed. 481-1207. (A winter alternative is pro-vided by the Agua Caliente Racetrack in Tijuana, which offers horseracing on Saturdays and Sundays only. Call 011-52-66-862003 for more information.)

MIRAMAR AIRSHOW: This outdoor celebration of Ameri-can airpower, starring the Navy's Blue Angels, is held in late July each year at the Miramar Naval Air Station, made famous in the 1986 movie, *Top Gun*. Bring sun-screen, a chair, and a cooler. 537-1011.

SOUTHERN CALIFORNIA EXPOSITION: Also known as the Del Mar Fair, this annual event, which normally falls between mid-June and early July, brings over a million people to the 350-acre fairgrounds adjacent to the race-track, for midway rides, flower and livestock shows, free outdoor concerts, and more. 755-1161.

Other annual events include:

January. Martin Luther King, Jr., Parade. Downtown. 265-3472.
March. St. Patrick's Day Parade. Downtown. 299-7812.

April. Flower and Garden Show. Spreckels Park, Coronado. 435-1787.

San Diego Padres baseball season begins, continuing through October. Jack Murphy Stadium. 283-7294.

May. Memorial Day Weekend Ethnic Food Fair. House of Pacific Relations, Balboa Park. 239-0512.

Cinco de Mayo Celebration. Old Town. 296-3161.

Pacific Beach Neighborhood Block Party. Pacific Beach. 483-6666.

June. Old Globe Theatre Summer Season begins, continuing through October. 239-2255.

Ocean Beach Street Fair and Chili Cook-Off. Ocean Beach. 224-3443.

August. Hillcrest Cityfest. Uptown. 299-3330.

September. San Diego Chargers football season begins, continuing through December. Jack Murphy Stadium. 563-8281.

October. San Diego Gulls hockey season begins, continuing through April. San Diego Sports Arena. 225-7825.

San Diego Sockers soccer season begins, continuing through April. San Diego Sports Arena. 224-4625.

Oktoberfest bash. Various streets, La Mesa.

December. Candle-lit processions in Balboa Park and Old Town celebrate Swedish and Mexican Christmas traditions and folklore. 230-2001 or 237-6770.

Parade of Lights. San Diego Harbor. 222-0561.

Index